✓ IN 6/82   ⑧

AN OUTLINE OF PSYCHO-ANALYSIS

By SIGMUND FREUD

AN AUTOBIOGRAPHICAL STUDY

CIVILIZATION AND ITS DISCONTENTS

THE COMPLETE INTRODUCTORY LECTURES ON PSYCHOANALYSIS

THE EGO AND THE ID

JOKES AND THEIR RELATION TO THE UNCONSCIOUS

LEONARDO DA VINCI AND A MEMORY OF HIS CHILDHOOD

NEW INTRODUCTORY LECTURES ON PSYCHOANALYSIS

ON DREAMS

ON THE HISTORY OF THE PSYCHO-ANALYTIC MOVEMENT

AN OUTLINE OF PSYCHO-ANALYSIS

THE PROBLEM OF ANXIETY

THE PSYCHOPATHOLOGY OF EVERYDAY LIFE

THE QUESTION OF LAY ANALYSIS

TOTEM AND TABOO

An Outline
of
Psycho-Analysis

SIGMUND FREUD

Translated and Newly Edited by
JAMES STRACHEY

NEW YORK

W · W · NORTON & COMPANY · INC ·

CT

131.34
F889ou
1969
c.2

ISBN 0 393 01083 X CLOTH EDITION
ISBN 0 393 00151 2 PAPER EDITION

Copyright 1949 by W. W. Norton & Company, Inc. Copyright
© 1969 by The Institute of Psychoanalysis and Alix Strachey.
First published in German under the title of *Abriss der Psycho-
Analyse* 1940. *Library of Congress Catalog Card No. 72-108329.*
Printed in the United States of America.

4 5 6 7 8 9 0

CONTENTS

Editor's Note   ix

Preface   1

PART I   THE MIND AND ITS WORKINGS

   I The Psychical Apparatus   1
  II The Theory of the Instincts   5
 III The Development of the Sexual Function   9
 IV Psychical Qualities   14
   V Dream-Interpretation as an Illustration   22

PART II   THE PRACTICAL TASK

  VI The Technique of Psycho-Analysis   29
 VII An Example of Psycho-Analytic Work   40

PART III   THE THEORETICAL YIELD

VIII The Psychical Apparatus and the External World   52
 IX The Internal World   62

ADDENDA   65

LIST OF ABBREVIATIONS   66

BIBLIOGRAPHY AND AUTHOR INDEX   67

GENERAL INDEX   71

EDITOR'S NOTE

ABRISS DER PSYCHOANALYSE

(*a*) GERMAN EDITIONS:

1940   *Int. Z. Psychoanal. Imago*, **25**(1), 7–67.
1941   *G.W.*, **17**, 63–138.

(*b*) ENGLISH TRANSLATION:
An Outline of Psycho-Analysis

1940   *Int. J. Psycho-Anal.*, **21**(1), 27–82. (Tr. James Strachey.)
1949   London: Hogarth Press and Institute of Psycho-Analysis. Pp. ix + 84. (Revised reprint of above in book form.)
1949   New York: Norton. Pp. 127. (Reprint of above.)
1964   *S.E.*, **23**, 141–207. (Considerably revised version of above.)

The present translation is a corrected reprint of the *Standard Edition* version, with a few editorial additions.

When this work was first published, both in German and English, it was accompanied by two long extracts from Freud's contemporary fragment 'Some Elementary Lessons in Psycho-Analysis' (1940*b* [1938]). These extracts appeared as a footnote in Chapter IV of the German version (see p. 15 below) and as an appendix in the English one. The fragment from which the extracts were drawn was published in full soon afterwards (it appears in *S.E.*, **23**, 279), and the footnote and appendix were consequently omitted in the subsequent reprints of the present work.

By an unfortunate oversight, the author's 'Preface' (p. 1 below) was omitted from the *G.W.* reprint and is thus only to be found in German in the *Zeitschrift*. It should be remarked that Volume XVII of the *Gesammelte Werke*, which was the first of its volumes to be published (in 1941), was also issued simultaneously with a different title-page and binding, as *Schriften aus dem Nachlass* (Posthumous Writings).

The manuscript of this whole work is written out in an

unusually abbreviated form. In particular the third chapter ('The Development of the Sexual Function', p. 9) is for the most part greatly abbreviated, with the omission, for instance, of definite and indefinite articles and of many principal verbs—in what may be described as a telegraphic style. The German editors have, as they tell us, expanded these abbreviations. The general sense is not in doubt and, although the editing is at certain points a little free, it has seemed simplest to accept it and to translate the version supplied in the *Gesammelte Werke*.

Part I of the work was not given a title by the author. The German editors adopted for the purpose 'Die Natur des Psychischen' ('The Nature of the Psychical') which is a cross-heading in the contemporary fragment mentioned above, 'Some Elementary Lessons in Psycho-Analysis' (*S.E.*, **23**, 282). For the present edition a rather more general title has been devised.

There is some conflict as to when Freud began writing the *Outline*. According to Ernest Jones (1957, 255) 'he began it during the waiting time in Vienna'—which would mean April or May, 1938. The manuscript, however, bears on its opening page the date 'July 22', which confirms the statement of the German editors that the work was begun in July, 1938—that is to say, soon after Freud's arrival in London at the beginning of June. By early September he had written 63 sheets of the *Outline*, when his work on it was interrupted by his having to undergo a very serious operation, and he did not return to it again, though he began shortly afterwards on another expository work ('Some Elementary Lessons in Psycho-Analysis') but very soon broke this off as well.

Thus the *Outline* must be described as unfinished, but it is difficult to regard it as incomplete. The last chapter, it is true, is shorter than the rest and might well have gone on to a discussion of such things as the sense of guilt, though this had already been touched on in Chapter VI. In general, however, the question of how far and in what direction Freud would have proceeded with the book is an intriguing one, for the programme laid down by the author in his preface seems already to be reasonably well carried out.

In the long succession of Freud's expository works the *Outline* exhibits a unique character. The others are without exception aimed at explaining psycho-analysis to an outside public, a public with very varying degrees and types of general approach to Freud's subject, but always a relatively *ignorant* public. This cannot be said of the *Outline*. It should clearly be understood that this is not a book for beginners; it is something much more like a 'refresher course' for advanced students. The reader is everywhere expected to be familiar not only with Freud's general approach to psychology but with his findings and theories on quite detailed points. For instance, a couple of very short allusions to the part played by the memory traces of verbal sense impressions (pp. 19 and 56) would scarcely be intelligible to anyone unacquainted with a number of difficult arguments in the last chapter of *The Interpretation of Dreams* and in the final section of the metapsychological paper on 'The Unconscious'. And again, the very scanty remarks in two or three places on identification and its relation to abandoned love-objects (pp. 50 and 60) imply a knowledge at least of Chapter III of *The Ego and the Id*. But those who are already at home in Freud's writings will find this a most fascinating epilogue. New light is thrown on whatever he touches—the most fundamental theories or the most detailed clinical observations—and everything is discussed in the vocabulary of his very latest terminology. There are even occasional hints at entirely new developments, particularly in the later part of Chapter VIII, where the question of the splitting of the ego and its disavowal of portions of the external world as exemplified in the case of fetishism receives an enlarged consideration. All of this shows that at the age of 82 Freud still possessed an astonishing gift for making a fresh approach to what might have seemed well-worn topics. Nowhere else, perhaps, does his style reach a higher level of succinctness and lucidity. The whole work gives us a sense of freedom in its presentation which is perhaps to be expected in a master's last account of the ideas of which he was the creator.

Editorial additions, whether to the text or the footnotes, are printed in square brackets.

In the editions of Freud's works published by W. W. Norton & Company Inc., the page numbers are the same as those in the Standard Edition for the following books:— *Jokes* (1905c), *Totem and Taboo* (1912–13), *Introductory Lectures* (1916–17), *The Ego and the Id* (1923b), the separate edition of *New Introductory Lectures* (1933a).

EDITORIAL NOTE

Since the original publication of the English translations of Freud's works there has appeared the new authoritative text of *The Standard Edition of the Complete Psychological Works of Sigmund Freud*, translated from the German under the general editorship of James Strachey, in collaboration with Anna Freud, assisted by Alix Strachey, Alan Tyson and Angela Richards. The Institute of Psycho-Analysis therefore thought it would be desirable to use this new text when reprinting the International Psycho-Analytical Library edition as the stocks of these began to get low. With the generous co-operation of Mr. Ernst Freud of Sigmund Freud Copyrights Ltd., Mrs. Alix Strachey and the Hogarth Press this aim has been achieved, and now as it becomes necessary to reprint any of Freud's works they are appearing in new editions in the International Psycho-Analytical Library with the text of *The Standard Edition*.

The present edition of Freud's *An Outline of Psycho-Analysis* contains the completely revised and fully annotated text of *The Standard Edition*. A bibliography and index have been provided and the volume has been prepared for publication by Angela Richards.

It is the hope of the Publications Committee that these revised texts with their annotations will be useful to the growing number of students and readers of psycho-analysis.

M. Masud R. Khan
*Editor, The International
Psycho-Analytical Library*

AN OUTLINE OF PSYCHO-ANALYSIS

PREFACE

THE aim of this brief work is to bring together the tenets of psycho-analysis and to state them, as it were, dogmatically—in the most concise form and in the most unequivocal terms. Its intention is naturally not to compel belief or to arouse conviction.

The teachings of psycho-analysis are based on an incalculable number of observations and experiences, and only someone who has repeated those observations on himself and on others is in a position to arrive at a judgement of his own upon it.

PART I

THE MIND AND ITS WORKINGS

CHAPTER I

THE PSYCHICAL APPARATUS

PSYCHO-ANALYSIS makes a basic assumption, the discussion of which is reserved to philosophical thought but the justification for which lies in its results. We know two kinds of things about what we call our psyche (or mental life): firstly, its bodily organ and scene of action, the brain (or nervous system) and, on the other hand, our acts of consciousness, which are immediate data and cannot be further explained by any sort of description. Everything that lies between is unknown to us, and the data do not include any direct relation between these two terminal points of our knowledge. If it existed, it would at the most afford an exact localization of the processes of consciousness and would give us no help towards understanding them.

Our two hypotheses start out from these ends or beginnings of our knowledge. The first is concerned with localization.[1] We assume that mental life is the function of an apparatus to which we ascribe the characteristics of being extended in space and of being made up of several portions—which we imagine, that is, as resembling a telescope or microscope or something of the kind. Notwithstanding some earlier attempts in the same direction, the consistent working-out of a conception such as this is a scientific novelty.

We have arrived at our knowledge of this psychical apparatus by studying the individual development of human beings. To the oldest of these psychical provinces or agencies we give the name of *id*. It contains everything that is inherited, that is present at birth, that is laid down in the constitution—above all, therefore, the instincts, which originate from the somatic organization and which find a first psychical expression here [in the id] in forms unknown to us.[2]

Under the influence of the real external world around us, one portion of the id has undergone a special development. From what was originally a cortical layer, equipped with the organs for receiving stimuli and with arrangements for acting as a protective shield against stimuli, a special organization has arisen which henceforward acts as an intermediary between the id and the external world. To this region of our mind we have given the name of *ego*.

Here are the principal characteristics of the ego. In consequence of the pre-established connection between sense perception and muscular action, the ego has voluntary movement at its command. It has the task of self-preservation. As regards *external* events, it performs that task by becoming aware of stimuli, by storing up experiences about them (in the memory), by avoiding excessively strong stimuli (through flight), by dealing with moderate stimuli (through adaptation) and finally by learning to bring about expedient changes in the external world to its own advantage (through activity). As regards *internal* events, in

---

[1] [The second is stated on p. 15 below.]

[2] This oldest portion of the psychical apparatus remains the most important throughout life; moreover, the investigations of psycho-analysis started with it.

relation to the id, it performs that task by gaining control over the demands of the instincts, by deciding whether they are to be allowed satisfaction, by postponing that satisfaction to times and circumstances favourable in the external world or by suppressing their excitations entirely. It is guided in its activity by consideration of the tensions produced by stimuli, whether these tensions are present in it or introduced into it. The raising of these tensions is in general felt as *unpleasure* and their lowering as *pleasure*. It is probable, however, that what is felt as pleasure or unpleasure is not the *absolute* height of this tension but something in the rhythm of the changes in them. The ego strives after pleasure and seeks to avoid unpleasure. An increase in unpleasure that is expected and foreseen is met by a *signal of anxiety*; the occasion of such an increase, whether it threatens from without or within, is known as a *danger*. From time to time the ego gives up its connection with the external world and withdraws into the state of sleep, in which it makes far-reaching changes in its organization. It is to be inferred from the state of sleep that this organization consists in a particular distribution of mental energy.

The long period of childhood, during which the growing human being lives in dependence on his parents, leaves behind it as a precipitate the formation in his ego of a special agency in which this parental influence is prolonged. It has received the name of *super-ego*. In so far as this super-ego is differentiated from the ego or is opposed to it, it constitutes a third power which the ego must take into account.

An action by the ego is as it should be if it satisfies simultaneously the demands of the id, of the super-ego and of reality—that is to say, if it is able to reconcile their demands with one another. The details of the relation between the ego and the super-ego become completely intelligible when they are traced back to the child's attitude to its parents. This parental influence of course includes in its operation not only the personalities of the actual parents but also the family, racial and national traditions handed on through them, as well as the demands of the immediate social *milieu* which they represent. In the same way, the super-ego, in the course of an individual's development, receives contributions from later successors and substitutes of his parents, such as teachers and models in public life of admired social ideals. It will be observed that, for all their fundamental difference, the id and the super-ego have one thing in common: they both represent the influences of the past—the id the influence of heredity, the super-ego the influence, essentially, of what is taken over from other people—whereas the ego is principally determined by the individual's own experience, that is by accidental and contemporary events.

This general schematic picture of a psychical apparatus may be supposed to apply as well to the higher animals which resemble man mentally. A super-ego must be presumed to be present wherever, as is the case with man, there is a long period of dependence in childhood. A distinction between ego and id is an unavoidable assumption. Animal psychology has not yet taken in hand the interesting problem which is here presented.

CHAPTER II

THE THEORY OF THE INSTINCTS

THE power of the id expresses the true purpose of the individual organism's life. This consists in the satisfaction of its innate needs. No such purpose as that of keeping itself alive or of protecting itself from dangers by means of anxiety can be attributed to the id. That is the task of the ego, whose business it also is to discover the most favourable and least perilous method of obtaining satisfaction, taking the external world into account. The super-ego may bring fresh needs to the fore, but its main function remains the limitation of satisfactions.

The forces which we assume to exist behind the tensions caused by the needs of the id are called *instincts*. They represent the somatic demands upon the mind. Though they are the ultimate cause of all activity, they are of a conservative nature; the state, whatever it may be, which an organism has reached gives rise to a tendency to re-establish that state so soon as it has been abandoned. It is thus possible to distinguish an indeterminate number of instincts, and in common practice this is in fact done. For us, however, the important question arises whether it may not be possible to trace all these numerous instincts back to a few basic ones. We have found that instincts can change their aim (by displacement) and also that they can replace one another—the energy of one instinct passing over to another. This latter process is still insufficiently understood. After long hesitancies and vacillations we have decided to assume the existence of only two basic instincts, *Eros* and *the destructive instinct*. (The contrast between the instincts of self-preservation and the preservation of the species, as well as the contrast between ego-love and object-love, fall within Eros.) The aim of the first of these basic instincts is to establish ever greater unities and to preserve them thus—in short, to bind together; the aim of the second is, on the contrary, to undo connections and so to destroy things. In the case of the destructive instinct we may suppose that its final aim is to lead what is living into an inorganic state. For this reason we also call it the *death instinct*. If we assume that living things came later than inani-

5

mate ones and arose from them, then the death instinct fits in with the formula we have proposed to the effect that instincts tend towards a return to an earlier state. In the case of Eros (or the love instinct) we cannot apply this formula. To do so would presuppose that living substance was once a unity which had later been torn apart and was now striving towards re-union.[1]

In biological functions the two basic instincts operate against each other or combine with each other. Thus, the act of eating is a destruction of the object with the final aim of incorporating it, and the sexual act is an act of aggression with the purpose of the most intimate union. This concurrent and mutually opposing action of the two basic instincts gives rise to the whole variegation of the phenomena of life. The analogy of our two basic instincts extends from the sphere of living things to the pair of opposing forces—attraction and repulsion—which rule in the inorganic world.[2]

Modifications in the proportions of the fusion between the instincts have the most tangible results. A surplus of sexual aggressiveness will turn a lover into a sex-murderer, while a sharp diminution in the aggressive factor will make him bashful or impotent.

There can be no question of restricting one or the other of the basic instincts to one of the provinces of the mind. They must necessarily be met with everywhere. We may picture an initial state as one in which the total available energy of Eros, which henceforward we shall speak of as 'libido', is present in the still undifferentiated ego-id[3] and serves to neutralize the destructive

[1] Creative writers have imagined something of the sort, but nothing like it is known to us from the actual history of living substance. [Freud no doubt had in mind among other writings Plato's *Symposium*, which he had quoted in this connection in *Beyond the Pleasure Principle* (1920g), *Standard Ed.*, **18**, 57–8, and to which he had alluded earlier still, in the first of the *Three Essays on the Theory of Sexuality* (1905d) *Standard Ed.*, **7**, 136.—*I.P.L.*, **4**, 51–2, and **57**, 2.]

[2] This picture of the basic forces or instincts, which still arouses much opposition among analysts, was already familiar to the philosopher Empedocles of Acragas. [Freud had discussed Empedocles and his theories at some length in Section VI of his paper on 'Analysis Terminable and Interminable' (1937c), *S.E.*, **23**, 245. He had included a reference to the dual forces operating in physics in his open letter to Einstein, *Why War?* (1933b), *Standard Ed.*, **22**, 209, as well as in Lecture XXXII of the *New Introductory Lectures* (1933a), ibid., 103.]

[3] [See footnote, p. 8 below.]

tendencies which are simultaneously present. (We are without a term analogous to 'libido' for describing the energy of the destructive instinct.) At a later stage it becomes relatively easy for us to follow the vicissitudes of the libido, but this is more difficult with the destructive instinct.

So long as that instinct operates internally, as a death instinct, it remains silent; it only comes to our notice when it is diverted outwards as an instinct of destruction. It seems to be essential for the preservation of the individual that this diversion should occur; the muscular apparatus serves this purpose. When the super-ego is established, considerable amounts of the aggressive instinct are fixated in the interior of the ego and operate there self-destructively. This is one of the dangers to health by which human beings are faced on their path to cultural development. Holding back aggressiveness is in general unhealthy and leads to illness (to mortification[1]). A person in a fit of rage will often demonstrate how the transition from aggressiveness that has been prevented to self-destructiveness is brought about by diverting the aggressiveness against himself: he tears his hair or beats his face with his fists, though he would evidently have preferred to apply this treatment to someone else. Some portion of self-destructiveness remains within, whatever the circumstances; till at last it succeeds in killing the individual, not, perhaps, until his libido has been used up or fixated in a disadvantageous way. Thus it may in general be suspected that the *individual* dies of his internal conflicts but that the *species* dies of its unsuccessful struggle against the external world if the latter changes in a fashion which cannot be adequately dealt with by the adaptations which the species has acquired.

It is hard to say anything of the behaviour of the libido in the id and in the super-ego. All that we know about it relates to the ego, in which at first the whole available quota of libido is stored up. We call this state absolute, primary *narcissism*. It lasts till the ego begins to cathect the ideas of objects with libido, to transform narcissistic libido into object-libido. Throughout the whole of life the ego remains the great reservoir from which libidinal cathexes are sent out to objects and into which they are also once more withdrawn, just as an amoeba

---

[1] ['*Kränkung*' means literally 'making ill'. This same point, including the verbal one, was made by Freud in a lecture on hysteria delivered forty-five years previously. See Freud, 1893*h*, *Standard Ed.*, **3**, 37.]

behaves with its pseudopodia.[1] It is only when a person is completely in love that the main quota of libido is transferred on to the object and the object to some extent takes the place of the ego. A characteristic of the libido which is important in life is its *mobility*, the facility with which it passes from one object to another. This must be contrasted with the *fixation* of the libido to particular objects, which often persists throughout life.

There can be no question but that the libido has somatic sources, that it streams to the ego from various organs and parts of the body. This is most clearly seen in the case of that portion of the libido which, from its instinctual aim, is described as sexual excitation. The most prominent of the parts of the body from which this libido arises are known by the name of 'erotogenic zones', though in fact the whole body is an erotogenic zone of this kind. The greater part of what we know about Eros —that is to say, about its exponent, the libido—has been gained from a study of the sexual function, which, indeed, on the prevailing view, even if not according to our theory, coincides with Eros. We have been able to form a picture of the way in which the sexual urge, which is destined to exercise a decisive influence on our life, gradually develops out of successive contributions from a number of component instincts, which represent particular erotogenic zones.

[1] [Some discussion of this passage, and of part of another one on p. 6 above, will be found in Appendix B to *The Ego and the Id* (1923*b*), *Standard Ed.*, **19**, 64–5; *I.P.L.*, **12**, 54–5; *N.*, 64–5.]

THE DEVELOPMENT OF THE SEXUAL FUNCTION

ACCORDING to the prevailing view human sexual life consists essentially in an endeavour to bring one's own genitals into contact with those of someone of the opposite sex. With this are associated, as accessory phenomena and introductory acts, kissing this extraneous body, looking at it and touching it. This endeavour is supposed to make its appearance at puberty—that is, at the age of sexual maturity—and to serve the purposes of reproduction. Nevertheless, certain facts have always been known which do not fit into the narrow framework of this view. (1) It is a remarkable fact that there are people who are only attracted by individuals of their own sex and by their genitals. (2) It is equally remarkable that there are people whose desires behave exactly like sexual ones but who at the same time entirely disregard the sexual organs or their normal use; people of this kind are known as 'perverts'. (3) And lastly it is a striking thing that some children (who are on that account regarded as degenerate) take a very early interest in their genitals and show signs of excitation in them.

It may well be believed that psycho-analysis provoked astonishment and denials when, partly on the basis of these three neglected facts, it contradicted all the popular opinions on sexuality. Its principal findings are as follows:

(*a*) Sexual life does not begin only at puberty, but starts with plain manifestations soon after birth.

(*b*) It is necessary to distinguish sharply between the concepts of 'sexual' and 'genital'. The former is the wider concept and includes many activities that have nothing to do with the genitals.

(*c*) Sexual life includes the function of obtaining pleasure from zones of the body—a function which is subsequently brought into the service of reproduction. The two functions often fail to coincide completely.

[1] [An expanded version of the original. See the Editor's Note, p. x above.]

The chief interest is naturally focused on the first of these assertions, the most unexpected of all. It has been found that in early childhood there are signs of bodily activity to which only an ancient prejudice could deny the name of sexual and which are linked to psychical phenomena that we come across later in adult erotic life—such as fixation to particular objects, jealousy, and so on. It is further found, however, that these phenomena which emerge in early childhood form part of an ordered course of development, that they pass through a regular process of increase, reaching a climax towards the end of the fifth year, after which there follows a lull. During this lull progress is at a standstill and much is unlearnt and there is much recession. After the end of this period of latency, as it is called, sexual life advances once more with puberty; we might say that it has a second efflorescence. And here we come upon the fact that the onset of sexual life is *diphasic*, that it occurs in two waves—something that is unknown except in man and evidently has an important bearing on hominization. [See p. 65 below.][1] It is not a matter of indifference that the events of this early period, except for a few residues, fall a victim to *infantile amnesia*. Our views on the aetiology of the neuroses and our technique of analytic therapy are derived from these conceptions; and our tracing of the developmental processes in this early period has also provided evidence for yet other conclusions.

The first organ to emerge as an erotogenic zone and to make libidinal demands on the mind is, from the time of birth onwards, the mouth. To begin with, all psychical activity is

[1] Cf. the suggestion that man is descended from a mammal which reached sexual maturity at the age of five, but that some major external influence was brought to bear on the species and at that point interrupted the straight course of development of sexuality. Other transformations in the sexual life of man as compared with that of animals might be connected with this—such as the abolition of the periodicity of the libido and the exploitation of the part played by menstruation in the relation between the sexes. [The idea of there being a connection between the latency period and the glacial epoch was first made many years earlier by Ferenczi (1913). Freud referred to it with a good deal of caution in *The Ego and the Id* (1923*b*), *S.E.*, **19**, 35; *I.P.L.*, **12**, 25 and again, with more acquiescence, in *Inhibitions, Symptoms and Anxiety* (1926*d*), *S.E.*, **20**, 155; *I.P.L.*, **28**, 69. The question of the cessation of periodicity in the sexual function was discussed at some length in two footnotes to Chapter IV of *Civilization and its Discontents* (1930*a*), *S.E.*, **21**, 99–100 and 105–7; *I.P.L.*, **17**, 36–7 and 42–4; *N.*, 46–7 and 52–4.]

concentrated on providing satisfaction for the needs of that zone. Primarily, of course, this satisfaction serves the purpose of self-preservation by means of nourishment; but physiology should not be confused with psychology. The baby's obstinate persistence in sucking gives evidence at an early stage of a need for satisfaction which, though it originates from and is instigated by the taking of nourishment, nevertheless strives to obtain pleasure independently of nourishment and for that reason may and should be termed *sexual*.

During this oral phase sadistic impulses already occur sporadically along with the appearance of the teeth. Their extent is far greater in the second phase, which we describe as the sadistic-anal one, because satisfaction is then sought in aggression and in the excretory function. Our justification for including aggressive urges under the libido is based on the view that sadism is an instinctual fusion of purely libidinal and purely destructive urges, a fusion which thenceforward persists uninterruptedly.[1]

The third phase is that known as the phallic one, which is, as it were, a forerunner of the final form taken by sexual life and already much resembles it. It is to be noted that it is not the genitals of both sexes that play a part at this stage, but only the male ones (the phallus). The female genitals long remain unknown: in children's attempts to understand the sexual processes they pay homage to the venerable cloacal theory—a theory which has a genetic justification.[2]

With the phallic phase and in the course of it the sexuality of early childhood reaches its height and approaches its dissolution. Thereafter boys and girls have different histories. Both have begun to put their intellectual activity at the service of sexual researches; both start off from the premiss of the universal presence of the penis. But now the paths of the sexes diverge.

[1] The question arises whether the satisfaction of purely destructive instinctual impulses can be felt as pleasure, whether pure destructiveness without any libidinal admixture occurs. Satisfaction of the death instinct remaining in the ego seems not to produce feelings of pleasure, though masochism represents a fusion which is entirely analogous to sadism.

[2] The occurrence of early vaginal excitations is often asserted. But it is most probable that what is in question are excitations in the clitoris— that is, in an organ analogous to the penis. This does not invalidate our right to describe the phase as phallic.

The boy enters the Oedipus phase; he begins to manipulate his penis and simultaneously has phantasies of carrying out some sort of activity with it in relation to his mother, till, owing to the combined effect of a threat of castration and the sight of the absence of a penis in females, he experiences the greatest trauma of his life and this introduces the period of latency with all its consequences. The girl, after vainly attempting to do the same as the boy, comes to recognize her lack of a penis or rather the inferiority of her clitoris, with permanent effects on the development of her character; as a result of this first disappointment in rivalry, she often begins by turning away altogether from sexual life.

It would be a mistake to suppose that these three phases succeed one another in a clear-cut fashion. One may appear in addition to another; they may overlap one another, may be present alongside of one another. In the early phases the different component instincts set about their pursuit of pleasure independently of one another; in the phallic phase there are the beginnings of an organization which subordinates the other urges to the primacy of the genitals and signifies the start of a co-ordination of the general urge towards pleasure into the sexual function. The complete organization is only achieved at puberty, in a fourth, genital phase. A state of things is then established in which (1) some earlier libidinal cathexes are retained, (2) others are taken into the sexual function as preparatory, auxiliary acts, the satisfaction of which produces what is known as fore-pleasure, and (3) other urges are excluded from the organization, and are either suppressed altogether (repressed) or are employed in the ego in another way, forming character-traits or undergoing sublimation with a displacement of their aims.

This process is not always performed faultlessly. Inhibitions in its development manifest themselves as the many sorts of disturbance in sexual life. When this is so, we find fixations of the libido to conditions in earlier phases, whose urge, which is independent of the normal sexual aim, is described as *perversion*. One such developmental inhibition, for instance, is homosexuality when it is manifest. Analysis shows that in every case a homosexual object-tie was present and in most cases persisted in a *latent* condition. The situation is complicated by the fact that as a rule the processes necessary for bringing about a normal outcome are not completely present or absent, but *partially* present, so that the final result remains dependent on these *quantitative* relations. In these circumstances the genital organization is, it is true, attained, but it lacks those portions of the libido which have not advanced with the rest and have remained fixated to pregenital objects and aims. This weakening shows itself in a tendency, if there is an absence of genital satisfaction or if there are difficulties in the real external world, for the libido to hark back to its earlier pregenital cathexes (*regression*).

During the study of the sexual functions we have been able to gain a first, preliminary conviction, or rather a suspicion, of two discoveries which will later be found to be important over the whole of our field. Firstly, the normal and abnormal manifestations observed by us (that is, the phenomenology of the subject) need to be described from the point of view of their dynamics and economics (in our case, from the point of view of the quantitative distribution of the libido). And secondly, the aetiology of the disorders which we study is to be looked for in the individual's developmental history—that is to say, in his early life.

CHAPTER IV

PSYCHICAL QUALITIES

I HAVE described the structure of the psychical apparatus and the energies or forces which are active in it, and I have traced in a prominent example the way in which those energies (in the main, the libido) organize themselves into a physiological function which serves the purpose of the preservation of the species. There was nothing in all this to demonstrate the quite peculiar characteristic of what is psychical, apart, of course, from the empirical fact that this apparatus and these energies are the basis of the functions which we describe as our mental life. I will now turn to something which is uniquely characteristic of what is psychical, and which, indeed, according to a very widely held opinion, coincides with it to the exclusion of all else.

The starting-point for this investigation is provided by a fact without parallel, which defies all explanation or description—the fact of consciousness. Nevertheless, if anyone speaks of consciousness we know immediately and from our most personal experience what is meant by it.[1] Many people, both inside and outside [psychological] science, are satisfied with the assumption that consciousness alone is psychical; in that case nothing remains for psychology but to discriminate among psychical phenomena between perceptions, feelings, thought-processes and volitions. It is generally agreed, however, that these conscious processes do not form unbroken sequences which are complete in themselves; there would thus be no alternative left to assuming that there are physical or somatic processes which are concomitant with the psychical ones and which we should necessarily have to recognize as more complete than the psychical sequences, since some of them would have conscious processes parallel to them but others would not. If so, it of course becomes plausible to lay the stress in psychology on these somatic processes, to see in *them* the true essence of what is psychical and to look for some other assessment of the conscious

[1] One extreme line of thought, exemplified in the American doctrine of behaviourism, thinks it possible to construct a psychology which disregards this fundamental fact!

14

processes. The majority of philosophers, however, as well as many other people, dispute this and declare that the idea of something psychical being unconscious is self-contradictory.

But that is precisely what psycho-analysis is obliged to assert, and this is its second fundamental hypothesis [p. 2]. It explains the supposedly somatic concomitant phenomena as being what is truly psychical, and thus in the first instance disregards the quality of consciousness. It is not alone in doing this. Some thinkers (such as Theodor Lipps,[1] for instance) have asserted the same thing in the same words; and the general dissatisfaction with the usual view of what is psychical has resulted in an increasingly urgent demand for the inclusion in psychological thought of a concept of the unconscious, though this demand has taken such an indefinite and obscure form that it could have no influence on science.[2]

Now it would look as though this dispute between psycho-analysis and philosophy is concerned only with a trifling matter of definition—the question whether the name 'psychical' should be applied to one or another sequence of phenomena. In fact, however, this step has become of the highest significance. Whereas the psychology of consciousness never went beyond the broken sequences which were obviously dependent on something else, the other view, which held that the psychical is unconscious in itself, enabled psychology to take its place as a natural science like any other. The processes with which it is concerned are in themselves just as unknowable as those dealt with by other sciences, by chemistry or physics, for example; but it is possible to establish the laws which they obey and to follow their mutual relations and interdependences unbroken over long stretches—in short, to arrive at what is described as an 'understanding' of the field of natural phenomena in question. This cannot be effected without framing fresh hypotheses and creating fresh concepts; but these are not to be despised as evidence of embarrassment on our part but deserve on the contrary to be appreciated as an enrichment of science. They

[1] [Some account of Lipps (1851–1914) and Freud's relations with him is given in the Editor's Preface to Freud's book on jokes (1905c, *Standard Ed.*, **8**, 4–5).]

[2] [When this work was first published in 1940, a long footnote was inserted at this point in the German version. See the Editor's Note, p. ix above.]

can lay claim to the same value as approximations that belongs to the corresponding intellectual scaffolding found in other natural sciences, and we look forward to their being modified, corrected and more precisely determined as further experience is accumulated and sifted. So too it will be entirely in accordance with our expectations if the basic concepts and principles of the new science (instinct, nervous energy, etc.) remain for a considerable time no less indeterminate than those of the older sciences (force, mass, attraction, etc.).

Every science is based on observations and experiences arrived at through the medium of our psychical apparatus. But since *our* science has as its subject that apparatus itself, the analogy ends here. We make our observations through the medium of the same perceptual apparatus, precisely with the help of the breaks in the sequence of 'psychical' events: we fill in what is omitted by making plausible inferences and translating it into conscious material. In this way we construct, as it were, a sequence of conscious events complementary to the unconscious psychical processes. The relative certainty of our psychical science is based on the binding force of these inferences. Anyone who enters deeply into our work will find that our technique holds its ground against any criticism.

In the course of this work the distinctions which we describe as psychical qualities force themselves on our notice. There is no need to characterize what we call 'conscious': it is the same as the consciousness of philosophers and of everyday opinion. Everything else psychical is in our view 'the unconscious'. We are soon led to make an important division in this unconscious. Some processes become conscious easily; they may then cease to be conscious, but can become conscious once more without any trouble: as people say, they can be reproduced or remembered. This reminds us that consciousness is in general a highly fugitive state. What is conscious is conscious only for a moment. If our perceptions do not confirm this, the contradiction is only an apparent one; it is explained by the fact that the stimuli which lead to perception may persist for considerable periods, so that meanwhile the perception of them may be repeated. The whole position is made clear in connection with the conscious perception of our thought-processes: these too may persist for some time, but they may just as well pass in a flash. Everything unconscious that behaves in this way, that can thus easily exchange the unconscious state for the conscious one, is therefore preferably described as 'capable of becoming conscious' or as *preconscious*. Experience has taught us that there is hardly a psychical process, however complicated it may be, which cannot on occasion remain preconscious, even though as a rule it will, as we say, push its way forward into consciousness. There are other psychical processes and psychical material which have no such easy access to becoming conscious but must be inferred, recognized and translated into conscious form in the manner described. For such material we reserve the name of the unconscious proper.

Thus we have attributed three qualities to psychical processes: they are either conscious, preconscious or unconscious. The division between the three classes of material which possess these qualities is neither absolute nor permanent. What is preconscious becomes conscious, as we have seen, without any assistance from us; what is unconscious can, through our efforts, be made conscious, and in the process we may have a feeling that we are often overcoming very strong resistances. When we attempt to do this with someone else, we should not forget that the conscious filling-in of the gaps in his perceptions—the construction we are presenting him with—does not mean as yet that we have made the unconscious material in question conscious to him. All that is true so far is that the material is present in him in two records,[1] once in the conscious reconstruction he has been given, and besides this in its original unconscious state. Our continued efforts usually succeed eventually in making this unconscious material conscious to him himself, as a result of which the two records are brought to coincide. The amount of effort we have to use, by which we estimate the resistance against the material becoming conscious, varies in magnitude in individual cases. For instance, what comes about in an analytic treatment as a result of our efforts can also occur spon-

[1] [The German word translated by 'record' here is '*Fixierung*' used in exactly this sense in Chapter VII (B) of *The Interpretation of Dreams* (1900a), *S.E.*, 5, 539. Elsewhere Freud uses the term '*Niederschrift*'—e.g. in 'The Unconscious' (1915e), *Standard Ed.*, 14, 174, and as early as in a letter to Fliess, of December 6, 1896 (Freud 1950a, Letter 52)—which is translated there by 'registration'. It may be remarked that in *Moses and Monotheism* (1939a), which Freud had recently completed, he several times used the word '*Fixierung*' to describe the recording of a tradition. See, for example, *Standard Ed.*, 23, 62.]

taneously: material which is ordinarily unconscious can transform itself into preconscious material and then becomes conscious—a thing that happens to a large extent in psychotic states. From this we infer that the maintenance of certain internal resistances is a *sine qua non* of normality. A relaxation of resistances such as this, with a consequent pushing forward of unconscious material, takes place regularly in the state of sleep, and thus brings about a necessary precondition for the construction of dreams. Conversely, preconscious material can become temporarily inaccessible and cut off by resistances, as happens when something is temporarily forgotten or escapes the memory; or a preconscious thought can even be temporarily put back into the unconscious state, as seems to be a precondition in the case of jokes. We shall see that a similar transformation back of preconscious material or processes into the unconscious state plays a great part in the causation of neurotic disorders.

The theory of the three qualities of what is psychical, as described in this generalized and simplified manner, seems likely to be a source of limitless confusion rather than a help towards clarification. But it should not be forgotten that in fact it is not a theory at all but a first stock-taking of the facts of our observations, that it keeps as close to those facts as possible and does not attempt to explain them. The complications which it reveals may bring into relief the peculiar difficulties with which our investigations have to contend. It may be suspected, however, that we shall come to a closer understanding of this theory itself if we trace out the relations between the psychical qualities and the provinces or agencies of the psychical apparatus which we have postulated—though these relations too are far from being simple.

The process of something becoming conscious is above all linked with the perceptions which our sense organs receive from the external world. From the topographical point of view, therefore, it is a phenomenon which takes place in the outermost cortex of the ego. It is true that we also receive conscious information from the inside of the body—the feelings, which actually exercise a more peremptory influence on our mental life than external perceptions; moreover, in certain circumstances the sense organs themselves transmit feelings, sensations of pain, in addition to the perceptions specific to them. Since, however, these sensations (as we call them in contrast to conscious perceptions) also emanate from the terminal organs and since we regard all these as prolongations or offshoots of the cortical layer, we are still able to maintain the assertion made above [at the beginning of this paragraph]. The only distinction would be that, as regards the terminal organs of sensation and feeling, the body itself would take the place of the external world.

Conscious processes on the periphery of the ego and everything else in the ego unconscious—such would be the simplest state of affairs that we might picture. And such may in fact be the state that prevails in animals. But in men there is an added complication through which internal processes in the ego may also acquire the quality of consciousness. This is the work of the function of speech, which brings material in the ego into a firm connection with mnemic residues of visual, but more particularly of auditory, perceptions. Thenceforward the perceptual periphery of the cortical layer can be excited to a much greater extent from inside as well, internal events such as passages of ideas and thought-processes can become conscious, and a special device is called for in order to distinguish between the two possibilities—a device known as *reality-testing*. The equation 'perception = reality (external world)' no longer holds. Errors, which can now easily arise and do so regularly in dreams, are called *hallucinations*.

The inside of the ego, which comprises above all the thought-processes, has the quality of being preconscious. This is characteristic of the ego and belongs to it alone. It would not be correct, however, to think that connection with the mnemic residues of speech is a necessary precondition of the preconscious state. On the contrary, that state is independent of a connection with them, though the presence of that connection makes it safe to infer the preconscious nature of a process. The preconscious state, characterized on the one hand by having access to consciousness and on the other hand by its connection with the speech-residues, is nevertheless something peculiar, the nature of which is not exhausted by these two characteristics. The evidence for this is the fact that large portions of the ego, and particularly of the super-ego, which cannot be denied the characteristic of preconsciousness, none the less remain for the most part unconscious in the phenomenological sense of the word. We do not know why this must be so. We shall attempt presently to attack the problem of the true nature of the preconscious.

The sole prevailing quality in the id is that of being unconscious. Id and unconscious are as intimately linked as ego and preconscious: indeed, in the former case the connection is even more exclusive. If we look back at the developmental history of an individual and of his psychical apparatus, we shall be able to perceive an important distinction in the id. Originally, to be sure, everything was id; the ego was developed out of the id by the continual influence of the external world. In the course of this slow development certain of the contents of the id were transformed into the preconscious state and so taken into the ego; others of its contents remained in the id unchanged, as its scarcely accessible nucleus. During this development, however, the young and feeble ego put back into the unconscious state some of the material it had already taken in, dropped it, and behaved in the same way to some fresh impressions which it *might* have taken in, so that these, having been rejected, could leave a trace only in the id. In consideration of its origin we speak of this latter portion of the id as *the repressed*. It is of little importance that we are not always able to draw a sharp line between these two categories of contents in the id. They coincide approximately with the distinction between what was innately present originally and what was acquired in the course of the ego's development.

Having now decided upon the topographical dissection of the psychical apparatus into an ego and an id, with which the difference in quality between preconscious and unconscious runs parallel, and having agreed that this quality is to be regarded only as an *indication* of the difference and not as its essence, a further question faces us. What, if this is so, is the true nature of the state which is revealed in the id by the quality of being unconscious and in the ego by that of being preconscious and in what does the difference between them consist?

But of that we know nothing. And the profound obscurity of the background of our ignorance is scarcely illuminated by a few glimmers of insight. Here we have approached the still shrouded secret of the nature of the psychical. We assume, as other natural sciences have led us to expect, that in mental life some kind of energy is at work; but we have nothing to go upon which will enable us to come nearer to a knowledge of it by analogies with other forms of energy. We seem to recognize that nervous or psychical energy occurs in two forms, one freely mobile and another, by comparison, bound; we speak of cathexes and hypercathexes of psychical material, and even venture to suppose that a hypercathexis brings about a kind of synthesis of different processes—a synthesis in the course of which free energy is transformed into bound energy. Further than this we have not advanced. At any rate, we hold firmly to the view that the distinction between the unconscious and the preconscious state lies in dynamic relations of this kind, which would explain how it is that, whether spontaneously or with our assistance, the one can be changed into the other.

Behind all these uncertainties, however, there lies one new fact, whose discovery we owe to psycho-analytic research. We have found that processes in the unconscious or in the id obey different laws from those in the preconscious ego. We name these laws in their totality the *primary process*, in contrast to the *secondary process* which governs the course of events in the pre-conscious, in the ego. In the end, therefore, the study of psychical qualities has after all proved not unfruitful.

Chapter V

DREAM-INTERPRETATION AS AN ILLUSTRATION

An investigation of normal, stable states, in which the frontiers of the ego are safeguarded against the id by resistances (anti-cathexes) and have held firm, and in which the super-ego is not distinguished from the ego, because they work together harmoniously—an investigation of that kind would teach us little. The only thing that can help us are states of conflict and uproar, when the contents of the unconscious id have a prospect of forcing their way into the ego and into consciousness and the ego puts itself once more on the defensive against this invasion. It is only under these conditions that we can make such observations as will confirm or correct our statements about the two partners. Now, our nightly sleep is precisely a state of this sort, and for that reason psychical activity during sleep, which we perceive as dreams, is our most favourable object of study. In that way, too, we avoid the familiar reproach that we base our constructions of normal mental life on pathological findings; for dreams are regular events in the life of a normal person, however much their characteristics may differ from the productions of our waking life. Dreams, as everyone knows, may be confused, unintelligible or positively nonsensical, what they say may contradict all that we know of reality, and we behave in them like insane people, since, so long as we are dreaming, we attribute objective reality to the contents of the dream.

We find our way to the understanding ('interpretation') of a dream by assuming that what we recollect as the dream after we have woken up is not the true dream-process but only a *façade* behind which that process lies concealed. Here we have our distinction between the *manifest* content of a dream and the *latent* dream-thoughts. The process which produces the former out of the latter is described as the *dream-work*. The study of the dream-work teaches us by an excellent example the way in which unconscious material from the id (originally unconscious and repressed unconscious alike) forces its way into the ego, becomes preconscious and, as a result of the ego's opposition, undergoes the changes which we know as *dream-distortion*. There

22

are no features of a dream which cannot be explained in this way.

It is best to begin by pointing out that the formation of a dream can be provoked in two different ways. Either, on the one hand, an instinctual impulse which is ordinarily suppressed (an unconscious wish) finds enough strength during sleep to make itself felt by the ego, or, on the other hand, an urge left over from waking life, a preconscious train of thought with all the conflicting impulses attached to it, finds reinforcement during sleep from an unconscious element. In short, dreams may arise either from the id or from the ego. The mechanism of dream-formation is in both cases the same and so also is the necessary dynamic precondition. The ego gives evidence of its original derivation from the id by occasionally ceasing its functions and allowing a reversion to an earlier state of things. This is logically brought about by its breaking off its relations with the external world and withdrawing its cathexes from the sense organs. We are justified in saying that there arises at birth an instinct to return to the intra-uterine life that has been abandoned—an instinct to sleep. Sleep is a return of this kind to the womb. Since the waking ego governs motility, that function is paralysed in sleep, and accordingly a good part of the inhibitions imposed on the unconscious id become superfluous. The withdrawal or reduction of these 'anticathexes' thus allows the id what is now a harmless amount of liberty.

The evidence of the share taken by the unconscious id in the formation of dreams is abundant and convincing. (a) Memory is far more comprehensive in dreams than in waking life. Dreams bring up recollections which the dreamer has forgotten, which are inaccessible to him when he is awake. (b) Dreams make an unrestricted use of linguistic symbols, the meaning of which is for the most part unknown to the dreamer. Our experience, however, enables us to confirm their sense. They probably originate from earlier phases in the development of speech. (c) Memory very often reproduces in dreams impressions from the dreamer's early childhood of which we can definitely assert not only that they had been forgotten but that they had become unconscious owing to repression. That explains the help—usually indispensable—given us by dreams in the attempts we make during the analytic treatment of neuroses to reconstruct the dreamer's early life. (d) Furthermore, dreams bring to light material which cannot have originated either from the dreamer's adult life or from his forgotten childhood. We are obliged to regard it as part of the *archaic heritage* which a child brings with him into the world, before any experience of his own, influenced by the experiences of his ancestors. We find the counterpart of this phylogenetic material in the earliest human legends and in surviving customs. Thus dreams constitute a source of human prehistory which is not to be despised.

But what makes dreams so invaluable in giving us insight is the circumstance that, when the unconscious material makes its way into the ego, it brings its own modes of working along with it. This means that the preconscious thoughts in which the unconscious material has found its expression are handled in the course of the dream-work as though they were unconscious portions of the id; and, in the case of the alternative method of dream-formation, the preconscious thoughts which have obtained reinforcement from an unconscious instinctual impulse are brought down to the unconscious state. It is only in this way that we learn the laws which govern the passage of events in the unconscious and the respects in which they differ from the rules that are familiar to us in waking thought. Thus the dream-work is essentially an instance of the unconscious working-over of preconscious thought-processes. To take an analogy from history: invading conquerors govern a conquered country, not according to the judicial system which they find in force there, but according to their own. It is, however, an unmistakable fact that the outcome of the dream-work is a compromise. The ego-organization is not yet paralysed, and its influence is to be seen in the distortion imposed on the unconscious material and in what are often very ineffective attempts at giving the total result a form not too unacceptable to the ego (*secondary revision*). In our analogy this would be an expression of the continued resistance of the defeated people.

The laws that govern the passage of events in the unconscious, which come to light in this manner, are remarkable enough and suffice to explain most of what seems strange to us about dreams. Above all there is a striking tendency to *condensation*, an inclination to form fresh unities out of elements which in our waking thought we should certainly have kept separate. As a consequence of this, a single element of the manifest dream often stands for a whole number of latent dream-thoughts as though it were a combined allusion to all of them; and in general the compass of the manifest dream is extraordinarily small in comparison with the wealth of material from which it has sprung. Another peculiarity of the dream-work, not entirely independent of the former one, is the ease with which psychical intensities[1] (cathexes) are *displaced* from one element to another, so that it often happens that an element which was of little importance in the dream-thoughts appears as the clearest and accordingly most important feature of the manifest dream, and, *vice versa*, that essential elements of the dream-thoughts are represented in the manifest dream only by slight allusions. Moreover, as a rule the existence of quite insignificant points in common between two elements is enough to allow the dream-work to replace one by the other in all further operations. It will easily be imagined how greatly these mechanisms of condensation and displacement can increase the difficulty of interpreting a dream and of revealing the relations between the manifest dream and the latent dream-thoughts. From the evidence of the existence of these two tendencies to condensation and displacement our theory infers that in the unconscious id the energy is in a freely mobile state and that the id sets more store by the possibility of discharging quantities of excitation than by any other consideration;[2] and our theory makes use of these two peculiarities in defining the character of the primary process we have attributed to the id.

The study of the dream-work has taught us many other characteristics of the processes in the unconscious which are as remarkable as they are important; but we must only mention a few of them here. The governing rules of logic carry no weight in the unconscious; it might be called the Realm of the

---

[1] [A term very often used by Freud from the earliest times as an equivalent to psychical energy. See the Editor's Appendix to the first paper on the neuro-psychoses of defence (1894a), *Standard Ed.*, **3**, 66–7; also an Editor's footnote near the end of the paper on 'Female Sexuality' (1931b), ibid., **21**, 242–3.]

[2] An analogy may be seen in the behaviour of a non-commissioned officer who accepts a reprimand from his superior in silence but vents his anger on the first innocent private he comes across. [In this insistance by the id on discharging quantities of excitation we have an exact replica of what Freud in his *Project* of 1895 (Part I, Section 1) had described in quasi-neurological terms as the primary principle of neuronal activity: 'neurones tend to divest themselves of quantity'. (1950a, *S.E.*, **1**, 296.)]

Illogical. Urges with contrary aims exist side by side in the unconscious without any need arising for an adjustment between them. Either they have no influence whatever on each other, or, if they have, no decision is reached, but a compromise comes about which is nonsensical since it embraces mutually incompatible details. With this is connected the fact that contraries are not kept apart but treated as though they were identical, so that in the manifest dream any element may also have the meaning of its opposite. Certain philologists have found that the same held good in the most ancient languages and that contraries such as 'strong-weak', 'light-dark' and 'high-deep' were originally expressed by the same roots, until two different modifications of the primitive word distinguished between the' two meanings. Residues of this original double meaning seem to have survived even in a highly developed language like Latin in its use of words such as '*altus*' ('high' and 'deep') and '*sacer*' ('sacred' and 'infamous'). [Cf. p. 65 below.]

In view of the complication and ambiguity of the relations between the manifest dream and the latent content lying behind it, it is of course justifiable to ask how it is at all possible to deduce the one from the other and whether all we have to go on is a lucky guess, assisted perhaps by a translation of the symbols that occur in the manifest dream. It may be said in reply that in the great majority of cases the problem can be satisfactorily solved, but only with the help of the associations provided by the dreamer himself to the elements of the manifest content. Any other procedure is arbitrary and can yield no certain result. But the dreamer's associations bring to light intermediate links which we can insert in the gap between the two [between the manifest and latent content] and by aid of which we can reinstate the latent content of the dream and 'interpret' it. It is not to be wondered at if this work of interpretation (acting in a direction opposite to the dream-work) fails occasionally to arrive at complete certainty.

It remains for us to give a dynamic explanation of why the sleeping ego takes on the task of the dream-work at all. The explanation is fortunately easy to find. With the help of the unconscious, every dream that is in process of formation makes a demand upon the ego—for the satisfaction of an instinct, if the dream originates from the id; for the solution of a conflict, the removal of a doubt or the forming of an intention, if the dream originates from a residue of preconscious activity in waking life. The sleeping ego, however, is focused on the wish to maintain sleep; it feels this demand as a disturbance and seeks to get rid of the disturbance. The ego succeeds in doing this by what appears to be an act of compliance: it meets the demand with what is in the circumstances a harmless *fulfilment of a wish* and so gets rid of it. This replacement of the demand by the fulfilment of a wish remains the essential function of the dream-work. It may perhaps be worth while to illustrate this by three simple examples—a hunger dream, a dream of convenience and a dream prompted by sexual desire. A need for food makes itself felt in a dreamer during his sleep: he has a dream of a delicious meal and sleeps on. The choice, of course, was open to him either of waking up and eating something or of continuing his sleep. He decided in favour of the latter and satisfied his hunger by means of the dream—for the time being, at all events, for if his hunger had persisted he would have had to wake up nevertheless. Here is the second example. A sleeper had to wake up so as to be in time for his work at the hospital. But he slept on, and had a dream that he was already at the hospital—but as a patient, who has no need to get up. Or again, a desire becomes active during the night for the enjoyment of a forbidden sexual object, the wife of a friend of the sleeper. He has a dream of sexual intercourse—not, indeed, with this person but with someone else of the same name to whom he is in fact indifferent; or his struggle against the desire may find expression in his mistress remaining altogether anonymous.

Naturally, every case is not so simple. Especially in dreams which have originated from undealt-with residues of the previous day, and which have only obtained an unconscious reinforcement during the state of sleep, it is often no easy task to uncover the unconscious motive force and its wish-fulfilment; but we may assume that it is always there. The thesis that dreams are the fulfilments of wishes will easily arouse scepticism when it is remembered how many dreams have an actually distressing content or even wake the dreamer in anxiety, quite apart from the numerous dreams without any definite feeling-tone. But the objection based on anxiety dreams cannot be sustained against analysis. It must not be forgotten that dreams are invariably the product of a conflict, that they are a kind of compromise-structure. Something that is a satisfaction for the unconscious id may for that very reason be a cause of anxiety for the ego.

As the dream-work proceeds, sometimes the unconscious will press forward more successfully and sometimes the ego will defend itself with greater energy. Anxiety dreams are mostly those whose content has undergone the least distortion. If the demand made by the unconscious is too great for the sleeping ego to be in a position to fend it off by the means at its disposal, it abandons the wish to sleep and returns to waking life. We shall be taking every experience into account if we say that a dream is invariably an *attempt* to get rid of a disturbance of sleep by means of a wish-fulfilment, so that the dream is a guardian of sleep. The attempt may succeed more or less completely; it may also fail, and in that case the sleeper wakes up, apparently woken precisely by the dream. So, too, there are occasions when that excellent fellow the night-watchman, whose business it is to guard the little township's sleep, has no alternative but to sound the alarm and waken the sleeping townspeople.

I will close this discussion with a comment which will justify the length of time I have spent on the problem of the interpretation of dreams. Experience has shown that the unconscious mechanisms which we have come to know from our study of the dream-work and which gave us the explanation of the formation of dreams also help us to understand the puzzling symptoms which attract our interest to neuroses and psychoses. A conformity of such a kind cannot fail to excite high hopes in us.

PART II

THE PRACTICAL TASK

CHAPTER VI

THE TECHNIQUE OF PSYCHO-ANALYSIS

A DREAM, then, is a psychosis, with all the absurdities, delusions and illusions of a psychosis. A psychosis of short duration, no doubt, harmless, even entrusted with a useful function, introduced with the subject's consent and terminated by an act of his will. None the less it is a psychosis, and we learn from it that even so deep-going an alteration of mental life as this can be undone and can give place to the normal function. Is it too bold, then, to hope that it must also be possible to submit the dreaded spontaneous illnesses of mental life to our influence and bring about their cure?

We already know a number of things preliminary to such an undertaking. According to our hypothesis it is the ego's task to meet the demands raised by its three dependent relations— to reality, to the id and to the super-ego—and nevertheless at the same time to preserve its own organization and maintain its own autonomy. The necessary precondition of the pathological states under discussion can only be a relative or absolute weakening of the ego which makes the fulfilment of its tasks impossible. The severest demand on the ego is probably the keeping down of the instinctual claims of the id, to accomplish which it is obliged to maintain large expenditures of energy on anticathexes. But the demands made by the super-ego too may become so powerful and so relentless that the ego may be paralysed, as it were, in the face of its other tasks. We may suspect that, in the economic conflicts which arise at this point, the id and the super-ego often make common cause against the hard-pressed ego which tries to cling to reality in order to retain its normal state. If the other two become too strong, they succeed in loosening and altering the ego's organization, so that its proper relation to reality is disturbed or even brought to an end. We have seen it happen in dreaming: when the ego is detached from the reality of the external world, it slips down, under the influence of the internal world, into psychosis.

Our plan of cure is based on these discoveries. The ego is weakened by the internal conflict and we must go to its help. The position is like that in a civil war which has to be decided by the assistance of an ally from outside. The analytic physician and the patient's weakened ego, basing themselves on the real external world, have to band themselves together into a party against the enemies, the instinctual demands of the id and the conscientious demands of the super-ego. We form a pact with each other. The sick ego promises us the most complete candour —promises, that is, to put at our disposal all the material which its self-perception yields it; we assure the patient of the strictest discretion and place at his service our experience in interpreting material that has been influenced by the unconscious. Our knowledge is to make up for his ignorance and to give his ego back its mastery over lost provinces of his mental life. This pact constitutes the analytic situation.

No sooner have we taken this step than a first disappointment awaits us, a first warning against over-confidence. If the patient's ego is to be a useful ally in our common work, it must, however hard it may be pressed by the hostile powers, have retained a certain amount of coherence and some fragment of understanding for the demands of reality. But this is not to be expected of the ego of a psychotic; it cannot observe a pact of this kind, indeed it can scarcely enter into one. It will very soon have tossed us away and the help we offer it and sent us to join the portions of the external world which no longer mean anything to it. Thus we discover that we must renounce the idea of trying our plan of cure upon psychotics—renounce it perhaps for ever or perhaps only for the time being, till we have found some other plan better adapted for them.

There is, however, another class of psychical patients who clearly resemble the psychotics very closely—the vast number of people suffering severely from neuroses. The determinants of their illness as well as its pathogenic mechanisms must be the same or at least very similar. But their ego has proved more resistant and has become less disorganized. Many of them, in spite of their maladies and the inadequacies resulting from them, have been able to maintain themselves in real life.

These neurotics may show themselves ready to accept our help. We will confine our interest to *them* and see how far and by what methods we are able to 'cure' them.

With the neurotics, then, we make our pact: complete candour on one side and strict discretion on the other. This looks as though we were only aiming at the post of a secular father confessor. But there is a great difference, for what we want to hear from our patient is not only what he knows and conceals from other people; he is to tell us too what he does *not* know. With this end in view we give him a more detailed definition of what we mean by candour. We pledge him to obey the *fundamental rule* of analysis, which is henceforward to govern his behaviour towards us. He is to tell us not only what he can say intentionally and willingly, what will give him relief like a confession, but everything else as well that his self-observation yields him, everything that comes into his head, even if it is *disagreeable* for him to say it, even if it seems to him *unimportant* or actually *nonsensical*. If he can succeed after this injunction in putting his self-criticism out of action, he will present us with a mass of material—thoughts, ideas, recollections—which are already subject to the influence of the unconscious, which are often its direct derivatives, and which thus put us in a position to conjecture his repressed unconscious material and to extend, by the information we give him, his ego's knowledge of his unconscious.

But it is far from being the case that his ego is content to play the part of passively and obediently bringing us the material we require and of believing and accepting our translation of it. A number of other things happen, a few of which we might have foreseen but others of which are bound to surprise us. The most remarkable thing is this. The patient is not satisfied with regarding the analyst in the light of reality as a helper and adviser who, moreover, is remunerated for the trouble he takes and who would himself be content with some such role as that of a guide on a difficult mountain climb. On the contrary, the patient sees in him the return, the reincarnation, of some important figure out of his childhood or past, and consequently transfers on to him feelings and reactions which undoubtedly applied to this prototype. This fact of transference soon proves to be a factor of undreamt-of importance, on the one hand an instrument of irreplaceable value and on the other hand a source of serious dangers. This transference is *ambivalent*: it comprises positive (affectionate) as well as negative (hostile) attitudes towards the analyst, who as a rule is put in the place of one or other of the patient's parents, his father or mother. So long as it is positive it serves us admirably. It alters the whole analytic situation; it pushes to one side the patient's rational aim of becoming healthy and free from his ailments. Instead of it there emerges the aim of pleasing the analyst and of winning his applause and love. It becomes the true motive force of the patient's collaboration; his weak ego becomes strong; under its influence he achieves things that would ordinarily be beyond his power; he leaves off his symptoms and seems apparently to have recovered—merely for the sake of the analyst. The analyst may shamefacedly admit to himself that he set out on a difficult undertaking without any suspicion of the extraordinary powers that would be at his command.

Moreover, the relation of transference brings with it two further advantages. If the patient puts the analyst in the place of his father (or mother), he is also giving him the power which his super-ego exercises over his ego, since his parents were, as we know, the origin of his super-ego. The new super-ego now has an opportunity for a sort of *after-education* of the neurotic; it can correct mistakes for which his parents were responsible in educating him. But at this point a warning must be given against misusing this new influence. However much the analyst may be tempted to become a teacher, model and ideal for other people and to create men in his own image, he should not forget that that is not his task in the analytic relationship, and indeed that he will be disloyal to his task if he allows himself to be led on by his inclinations. If he does, he will only be repeating a mistake of the parents who crushed their child's independence by their influence, and he will only be replacing the patient's earlier dependence by a new one. In all his attempts at improving and educating the patient the analyst should respect his individuality. The amount of influence which he may legitimately allow himself will be determined by the degree of developmental inhibition present in the patient. Some neurotics have remained so infantile that in analysis too they can only be treated as children.

Another advantage of transference, too, is that in it the

patient produces before us with plastic clarity an important part of his life-story, of which he would otherwise have probably given us only an insufficient account. He acts it before us, as it were, instead of reporting it to us.

And now for the other side of the situation. Since the transference reproduces the patient's relation with his parents, it takes over the ambivalence of that relation as well. It almost inevitably happens that one day his positive attitude towards the analyst changes over into the negative, hostile one. This too is as a rule a repetition of the past. His obedience to his father (if it is his father that is in question), his courting of his father's favour, had its roots in an erotic wish directed towards him. Some time or other that demand will press its way forward in the transference as well and insist on being satisfied. In the analytic situation it can only meet with frustration. Real sexual relations between patients and analysts are out of the question, and even the subtler methods of satisfaction, such as the giving of preference, intimacy and so on, are only sparingly granted by the analyst. A rejection of this kind is taken as the occasion for the change-over; probably things happened in the same way in the patient's childhood.

The therapeutic successes that occurred under the sway of the positive transference are open to the suspicion of being of a *suggestive* nature. If the negative transference gains the upper hand, they are blown away like chaff before the wind. We observe with horror that all our trouble and labour hitherto have been in vain. Indeed, what we might have regarded as a permanent intellectual gain by the patient, his understanding of psycho-analysis and his reliance on its efficacy, suddenly vanish. He behaves like a child who has no power of judgement of his own but blindly believes anyone whom he loves and no one who is a stranger to him. The danger of these states of transference evidently lies in the patient's misunderstanding their nature and taking them for fresh real experiences instead of reflections of the past. If he (or she) becomes aware of the strong erotic desire that lies concealed behind the positive transference, he believes that he has fallen passionately in love; if the transference changes over, then he feels insulted and neglected, he hates the analyst as his enemy and is ready to abandon the analysis. In both these extreme cases he has forgotten the pact that he made at the beginning of the treatment and has become useless for continuing the common work. It is the analyst's task constantly to tear the patient out of his menacing illusion and to show him again and again that what he takes to be new real life is a reflection of the past. And lest he should fall into a state in which he is inaccessible to all evidence, the analyst takes care that neither the love nor the hostility reach an extreme height. This is effected by preparing him in good time for these possibilities and by not overlooking the first signs of them. Careful handling of the transference on these lines is as a rule richly rewarded. If we succeed, as we usually can, in enlightening the patient on the true nature of the phenomena of transference, we shall have struck a powerful weapon out of the hand of his resistance and shall have converted dangers into gains. For a patient never forgets again what he has experienced in the form of transference; it carries a greater force of conviction than anything he can acquire in other ways.

We think it most undesirable if the patient *acts* outside the transference instead of remembering. The ideal conduct for our purposes would be that he should behave as normally as possible outside the treatment and express his abnormal reactions only in the transference.

The method by which we strengthen the weakened ego has as a starting-point an extending of its self-knowledge. That is not, of course, the whole story but it is a first step. The loss of such knowledge signifies for the ego a surrender of power and influence; it is the first tangible sign that it is being hemmed in and hampered by the demands of the id and the super-ego. Accordingly, the first part of the help we have to offer is intellectual work on our side and encouragement to the patient to collaborate in it. This first kind of activity, as we know, is intended to pave the way to another, more difficult, task. We shall not lose sight of the dynamic element in this task, even during its preliminary stage. We gather the material for our work from a variety of sources—from what is conveyed to us by the information given us by the patient and by his free associations, from what he shows us in his transferences, from what we arrive at by interpreting his dreams and from what he betrays by his slips or *parapraxes*. All this material helps us to make constructions about what happened to him and has been forgotten as well as about what is happening in him now without his understanding it. But in all this we never fail to make a strict distinction between *our* knowledge and *his* knowledge. We avoid telling him at once things that we have often discovered at an early stage, and we avoid telling him the whole of what we think we have discovered. We reflect carefully over when we shall impart the knowledge of one of our constructions to him and we wait for what seems to us the suitable moment—which it is not always easy to decide. As a rule we put off telling him of a construction or explanation till he himself has so nearly arrived at it that only a single step remains to be taken, though that step is in fact the decisive synthesis. If we proceeded in another way and overwhelmed him with our interpretations before he was prepared for them, our information would either produce no effect or it would provoke a violent outbreak of *resistance* which would make the progress of our work more difficult or might even threaten to stop it altogether. But if we have prepared everything properly, it often happens that the patient will at once confirm our construction and himself recollect the internal or external event which he had forgotten. The more exactly the construction coincides with the details of what has been forgotten the easier will it be for him to assent. On that particular matter *our* knowledge will then have become *his* knowledge as well.

With the mention of resistance we have reached the second and more important part of our task. We have already learnt that the ego protects itself against the invasion of undesired elements from the unconscious and repressed id by means of anticathexes, which must remain intact if it is to function normally. The more hard-pressed the ego feels, the more convulsively it clings (as though in a fright) to these anticathexes, in order to protect what remains of itself from further irruptions. But this defensive purpose does not by any means accord with the aims of our treatment. What we desire, on the contrary, is that the ego, emboldened by the certainty of our help, shall dare to take the offensive in order to reconquer what has been lost. And it is here that we become aware of the strength of these anticathexes in the form of *resistances* to our work. The ego draws back in alarm from such undertakings, which seem dangerous and threaten unpleasure; it must be constantly encouraged and soothed if it is not to fail us. This resistance, which persists throughout the whole treatment and is renewed at every fresh piece of work, is known, not quite correctly, as the *resistance due to repression*. We shall find that it is not the only one that faces us. It is interesting to notice that in this situation the party-divisions are to some extent reversed: for the ego struggles against our instigation, while the unconscious, which is ordinarily our opponent, comes to our help, since it has a natural 'upward drive' and desires nothing better than to press forward across its settled frontiers into the ego and so to consciousness. The struggle which develops, if we gain our end and can induce the ego to overcome its resistances, is carried through under our direction and with our assistance. Its outcome is a matter of indifference: whether it results in the ego accepting, after a fresh examination, an instinctual demand which it has hitherto rejected, or whether it dismisses it once more, this time for good and all. In either case a permanent danger has been disposed of, the compass of the ego has been extended and a wasteful expenditure of energy has been made unnecessary.

The overcoming of resistances is the part of our work that requires the most time and the greatest trouble. It is worth while, however, for it brings about an advantageous alteration of the ego which will be maintained independently of the outcome of the transference and will hold good in life. We have also worked simultaneously at getting rid of the alteration of the ego which had been brought about under the influence of the unconscious; for whenever we have been able to detect any of its derivatives in the ego we have pointed out their illegitimate origin and have instigated the ego to reject them. It will be remembered that it was one of the necessary preconditions of our pact of assistance that any such alteration of the ego due to the intrusion of unconscious elements should not have gone beyond a certain amount.

The further our work proceeds and the more deeply our insight penetrates into the mental life of neurotics, the more clearly two new factors force themselves on our notice, which demand the closest attention as sources of resistance. Both of them are completely unknown to the patient, neither of them could be taken into account when our pact was made; nor do they arise from the patient's ego. They may both be embraced under the single name of 'need to be ill or to suffer', but they have different origins though in other respects they are of a kindred nature. The first of these two factors is the sense of guilt or consciousness of guilt, as it is called, though the patient does not feel it and is not aware of it. It is evidently the portion of the resistance contributed by a super-ego that has become particularly severe and cruel. The patient must not become well but must remain ill, for he deserves no better. This resistance does not actually interfere with our intellectual work, but it makes it inoperative; indeed, it often allows us to remove one form of neurotic suffering, but is ready at once to replace it by another, or perhaps by some somatic illness. The sense of guilt also explains the cure or improvement of severe neuroses which we occasionally observe after real misfortunes: all that matters is that the patient should be miserable—in what way is of no consequence. The uncomplaining resignation with which such people often put up with their hard fate is most remarkable, but also revealing. In warding off this resistance we are obliged to restrict ourselves to making it conscious and attempting to bring about the slow demolition of the hostile super-ego.

It is less easy to demonstrate the existence of another resistance, our means of combating which are specially inadequate. There are some neurotics in whom, to judge by all their reactions, the instinct of self-preservation has actually been reversed. They seem to aim at nothing other than self-injury and self-destruction. It is possible too that the people who in fact do in the end commit suicide belong to this group. It is to be assumed that in such people far-reaching defusions of instinct have taken place, as a result of which there has been a liberation of excessive quantities of the destructive instinct directed inwards. Patients of this kind are not able to tolerate recovery through our treatment and fight against it with all their strength. But we must confess that this is a case which we have not yet succeeded in completely explaining.

Let us once more glance over the situation which we have reached in our attempt at bringing help to the patient's neurotic ego. That ego is no longer able to fulfil the task set it by the external world (including human society). Not all of its experiences are at its disposal, a large proportion of its store of memories have escaped it. Its activity is inhibited by strict prohibitions from the super-ego, its energy is consumed in vain attempts at fending off the demands of the id. Beyond this, as a result of continuous irruptions by the id, its organization is impaired, it is no longer capable of any proper synthesis, it is torn by mutually opposed urges, by unsettled conflicts and by unsolved doubts. To start with, we get the patient's thus weakened ego to take part in the purely intellectual work of interpretation, which aims at provisionally filling the gaps in his mental assets, and to transfer to us the authority of his super-ego; we encourage it to take up the struggle over each individual demand made by the id and to conquer the resistances which arise in connection with it. At the same time we restore order in the ego by detecting the material and urges which have forced their way in from the unconscious, and expose them to criticism by tracing them back to their origin. We serve the patient in various functions, as an authority and a substitute for his parents, as a teacher and educator; and we have done the best for him if, as analysts, we raise the mental processes in his ego to a normal level, transform what has become unconscious and repressed into preconscious material and thus return it once more to the possession of his ego. On the patient's side a few rational factors work in our favour, such as the need for recovery which has its motive in his sufferings, and the intellectual interest that we may awaken in him in the theories and revelations of psycho-analysis; but of far greater force is the positive transference with which he meets us. Fighting against us, on the other hand, are the negative transference, the ego's resistance due to repression (that is, its unpleasure at having to lay itself open to the hard work imposed on it), the sense of guilt arising from its relation to the super-ego and the need to be ill due to deep-going changes in the economics of his[1] instincts. The share taken by the last two factors decides whether the case is to be regarded as slight or severe. Apart from these, a few other factors may be discerned as having a favourable or unfavourable bearing. A certain psychical inertia, a sluggishness of the libido, which is unwilling to abandon its fixations, cannot be welcome to us; the patient's capacity for sublimating his instincts plays a large part and so does his capacity for rising above the crude life of the instincts; so, too, does the relative power of his intellectual functions.

We shall not be disappointed, but, on the contrary, we shall find it entirely intelligible, if we reach the conclusion that the final outcome of the struggle we have engaged in depends on

[1] ['*Seiner.*' This can be either 'its' or 'his'; it seems much more likely to refer to the person as a whole rather than to the ego.]

quantitative relations—on the quota of energy we are able to mobilize in the patient to our advantage as compared with the sum of energy of the powers working against us. Here once again God is on the side of the big battalions. It is true that we do not always succeed in winning, but at least we can usually recognize why we have not won. Those who have been following our discussion only out of therapeutic interest will perhaps turn away in contempt after this admission. But here we are concerned with therapy only in so far as it works by psychological means; and for the time being we have no other. The future may teach us to exercise a direct influence, by means of particular chemical substances, on the amounts of energy and their distribution in the mental apparatus. It may be that there are other still undreamt-of possibilities of therapy. But for the moment we have nothing better at our disposal than the technique of psycho-analysis, and for that reason, in spite of its limitations, it should not be despised.

Chapter VII

AN EXAMPLE OF PSYCHO-ANALYTIC WORK

WE have arrived at a general acquaintance with the psychical apparatus, with the parts, organs and agencies of which it is composed, with the forces which operate in it and with the functions allotted to its parts. The neuroses and psychoses are the states in which disturbances in the functioning of the apparatus come to expression. We have chosen the neuroses as the subjects of our study because they alone seem accessible to the psychological methods of our intervention. While we are trying to influence them, we collect observations which give us a picture of their origin and of the manner in which they arise.

I will state in advance one of our chief findings before proceeding with my description. The neuroses (unlike infectious diseases, for instance) have no specific determinants. It would be idle to seek in them for pathogenic excitants. They shade off by easy transitions into what is described as the normal; and, on the other hand, there is scarcely any state recognized as normal in which indications of neurotic traits could not be pointed out. Neurotics have approximately the same innate dispositions as other people, they have the same experiences and they have the same tasks to perform. Why is it, then, that they live so much worse and with so much greater difficulty and, in the process, suffer more feelings of unpleasure, anxiety and pain?

We need not be at a loss to find an answer to this question. Quantitative *disharmonies* are what must be held responsible for the inadequacy and sufferings of neurotics. The determining cause of all the forms taken by human mental life, is, indeed, to be sought in the reciprocal action between innate dispositions and accidental experiences. Now a particular instinct may be too strong or too weak innately, or a particular capacity may be stunted or insufficiently developed in life. On the other hand, external impressions and experiences may make demands of differing strength on different people; and what one person's constitution can deal with may prove an unmanageable task for another's. These quantitative differences will determine the variety of the results.

We shall very soon feel, however, that this explanation is unsatisfactory: it is too general, it explains too much. The aetiology put forward applies to every case of mental suffering, misery and disablement, but not every such state can be termed neurotic. The neuroses have specific characteristics, they are miseries of a particular kind. So we must after all expect to find particular causes for them. Or we may adopt the supposition that, among the tasks with which mental life has to deal, there are a few on which it can especially easily come to grief; so that the peculiarity of the phenomena of neurosis, which are often so very remarkable, would follow from this without our needing to withdraw our earlier assertions. If it remains true that the neuroses do not differ in any essential respect from the normal, their study promises to yield us valuable contributions to our knowledge of the normal. It may be that we shall thus discover the 'weak points' in a normal organization.

The supposition we have just made finds confirmation. Analytic experiences teach us that there is in fact one instinctual demand attempts to deal with which most easily fail or succeed imperfectly and that there is one period of life which comes in question exclusively or predominantly in connection with the generation of a neurosis. These two factors—the nature of the instinct and the period of life concerned—call for separate consideration, although they are closely enough connected.

We can speak with a fair degree of certainty about the part played by the period of life. It seems that neuroses are acquired only in early childhood (up to the age of six), even though their symptoms may not make their appearance till much later. The childhood neurosis may become manifest for a short time or may even be overlooked. In every case the later neurotic illness links up with the prelude in childhood. It is possible that what are known as traumatic neuroses (due to excessive fright or severe somatic shocks, such as railway collisions, burial under falls of earth, and so on) are an exception to this: their relations to determinants in childhood have hitherto eluded investigation. There is no difficulty in accounting for this aetiological preference for the first period of childhood. The neuroses are, as we know, disorders of the ego; and it is not to be wondered at if the ego, so long as it is feeble, immature and incapable of resistance, fails to deal with tasks which it could cope with later on with the utmost ease. In these circumstances instinctual demands from within, no less than excitations from the external world, operate as 'traumas', particularly if they are met half-way by certain innate dispositions. The helpless ego fends them off by means of attempts at flight (*repressions*), which later turn out to be inefficient and which involve permanent restrictions on further development. The damage inflicted on the ego by its first experiences gives us the appearance of being dispropor-tionately great; but we have only to take as an analogy the differences in the results produced by the prick of a needle into a mass of cells in the act of cell-division (as in Roux's experi-ments) and into the fully grown animal which eventually develops out of them.[1] No human individual is spared such traumatic experiences; none escapes the repressions to which they give rise. These questionable reactions on the part of the ego may perhaps be indispensable for the attainment of another aim which is set for the same period of life: in the space of a few years the little primitive creature must turn into a civilized human being; he must pass through an immensely long stretch of human cultural development in an almost uncannily ab-breviated form. This is made possible by hereditary disposition; but it can almost never be achieved without the additional help of upbringing, of parental influence, which, as a precursor of the super-ego, restricts the ego's activity by prohibitions and punishments, and encourages or compels the setting-up of repressions. We must therefore not forget to include the influ-ence of civilization among the determinants of neurosis. It is easy, as we can see, for a barbarian to be healthy; for a civilized man the task is hard. The desire for a powerful, uninhibited ego may seem to us intelligible; but, as we are taught by the times we live in, it is in the profoundest sense hostile to civiliza-tion. And since the demands of civilization are represented by family upbringing, we must bear in mind the part played by this biological characteristic of the human species—the pro-longed period of its childhood dependence—in the aetiology of the neuroses.

As regards the other point—the specific instinctual factor—we come upon an interesting discrepancy between theory and

[1] [Wilhelm Roux (1850–1924) was one of the founders of experi-mental embryology.]

experience. Theoretically there is no objection to supposing that any sort of instinctual demand might occasion the same repressions and their consequences; but our observation shows us invariably, so far as we can judge, that the excitations that play this pathogenic part arise from the component instincts of sexual life. The symptoms of neuroses are, it might be said, without exception either a substitutive satisfaction of some sexual urge or measures to prevent such a satisfaction; and as a rule they are compromises between the two, of the kind that come about in accordance with the laws operating between contraries in the unconscious. The gap in our theory cannot at present be filled; our decision is made more difficult by the fact that most of the urges of sexual life are not of a purely erotic nature but have arisen from alloys of the erotic instinct with portions of the destructive instinct. But it cannot be doubted that the instincts which manifest themselves physiologically as sexuality play a prominent, unexpectedly large part in the causation of the neuroses—whether it is an exclusive one remains to be decided. It must also be borne in mind that in the course of cultural development no other function has been so energetically and extensively repudiated as precisely the sexual one. Theory must rest satisfied with a few hints that betray a deeper connection: the fact that the first period of childhood, during which the ego begins to be differentiated from the id, is also the period of the early sexual efflorescence which is brought to an end by the period of latency; that it can hardly be a matter of chance that this momentous early period subsequently falls a victim to infantile amnesia; and lastly, that biological changes in sexual life (such as the function's diphasic onset which we have already mentioned, the disappearance of the periodic character of sexual excitation and the transformation in the relation between female menstruation and male excitation)—that these innovations in sexuality must have been of high importance in the evolution of animals into man. It is left for the science of the future to bring these still isolated data together into a new understanding. It is not in psychology but in biology that there is a gap here. We shall not be wrong, perhaps, in saying that the weak point in the ego's organization seems to lie in its attitude to the sexual function, as though the biological antithesis between self-preservation and the preservation of the species had found a psychological expression at that point.

Analytic experience has convinced us of the complete truth of the assertion so often to be heard that the child is psychologically father to the adult and that the events of his first years are of paramount importance for his whole later life. It will thus be of special interest to us if there is something that may be described as the central experience of this period of childhood. Our attention is first attracted by the effects of certain influences which do not apply to all children, though they are common enough—such as the sexual abuse of children by adults, their seduction by other children (brothers or sisters) slightly their seniors, and, what we should not expect, their being deeply stirred by seeing or hearing at first hand sexual behaviour between adults (their parents) mostly at a time at which one would not have thought they could either be interested in or understand any such impressions, or be capable of remembering them later. It is easy to confirm the extent to which such experiences arouse a child's susceptibility and force his own sexual urges into certain channels from which they cannot afterwards depart. Since these impressions are subjected to repression either at once or as soon as they seek to return as memories, they constitute the determinant for the neurotic compulsion which will subsequently make it impossible for the ego to control the sexual function and will probably cause it to turn away from that function permanently. If this latter reaction occurs, the result will be a neurosis; if it is absent, a variety of perversions will develop, or the function, which is of immense importance not only for reproduction but also for the entire shaping of life, will become totally unmanageable.

However instructive cases of this kind may be, a still higher degree of interest must attach to the influence of a situation which every child is destined to pass through and which follows inevitably from the factor of the prolonged period during which a child is cared for by other people and lives with his parents. I am thinking of the *Oedipus complex*, so named because its essential substance is to be found in the Greek legend of King Oedipus, which has fortunately been preserved for us in a version by a great dramatist. The Greek hero killed his father and took his mother to wife. That he did so unwittingly, since he did not know them as his parents, is a deviation from the analytic facts which we can easily understand and which, indeed, we shall recognize as inevitable.

At this point we must give separate accounts of the development of boys and girls (of males and females), for it is now that the difference between the sexes finds psychological expression for the first time. We are faced here by the great enigma of the biological fact of the duality of the sexes: it is an ultimate fact for our knowledge, it defies every attempt to trace it back to something else. Psycho-analysis has contributed nothing to clearing up this problem, which clearly falls wholly within the province of biology. In mental life we only find reflections of this great antithesis; and their interpretation is made more difficult by the fact, long suspected, that no individual is limited to the modes of reaction of a single sex but always finds some room for those of the opposite one, just as his body bears, alongside of the fully developed organs of one sex, atrophied and often useless rudiments of those of the other. For distinguishing between male and female in mental life we make use of what is obviously an inadequate empirical and conventional equation: we call everything that is strong and active male, and everything that is weak and passive female. This fact of psychological bisexuality, too, embarrasses all our enquiries into the subject and makes them harder to describe.

A child's first erotic object is the mother's breast that nourishes it; love has its origin in attachment to the satisfied need for nourishment. There is no doubt that, to begin with, the child does not distinguish between the breast and its own body; when the breast has to be separated from the body and shifted to the '*outside*' because the child so often finds it absent, it carries with it as an '*object*' a part of the original narcissistic libidinal cathexis. This first object is later completed into the person of the child's mother, who not only nourishes it but also looks after it and thus arouses in it a number of other physical sensations, pleasurable and unpleasurable. By her care of the child's body she becomes its first seducer. In these two relations lies the root of a mother's importance, unique, without parallel, established unalterably for a whole lifetime as the first and strongest love-object and as the prototype of all later love-relations—for both sexes. In all this the phylogenetic foundation has so much the upper hand over personal accidental experience that it makes no difference whether a child has really sucked at the breast or has been brought up on the bottle and never enjoyed the tenderness of a mother's care. In both cases the child's development takes the same path; it may be that in the second case its later longing grows all the greater. And for however long it is fed at its mother's breast, it will always be left with a conviction after it has been weaned that its feeding was too short and too little.

This preface is not superfluous, for it can heighten our realization of the intensity of the Oedipus complex. When a boy (from the age of two or three) has entered the phallic phase of his libidinal development, is feeling pleasurable sensations in his sexual organ and has learnt to procure these at will by manual stimulation, he becomes his mother's lover. He wishes to possess her physically in such ways as he has divined from his observations and intuitions about sexual life, and he tries to seduce her by showing her the male organ which he is proud to own. In a word, his early awakened masculinity seeks to take his father's place with her; his father has hitherto in any case been an envied model to the boy, owing to the physical strength he perceives in him and the authority with which he finds him clothed. His father now becomes a rival who stands in his way and whom he would like to get rid of. If while his father is away he is allowed to share his mother's bed and if when his father returns he is once more banished from it, his satisfaction when his father disappears and his disappointment when he emerges again are deeply felt experiences. This is the subject of the Oedipus complex, which the Greek legend has translated from the world of a child's phantasy into pretended reality. Under the conditions of our civilization it is invariably doomed to a frightening end.

The boy's mother has understood quite well that his sexual excitation relates to herself. Sooner or later she reflects that it is not right to allow it to continue. She thinks she is doing the correct thing in forbidding him to handle his genital organ. Her prohibition has little effect; at the most it brings about some modification in his method of obtaining satisfaction. At last his mother adopts the severest measures; she threatens to take away from him the thing he is defying her with. Usually, in order to make the threat more frightening and more credible, she delegates its execution to the boy's father, saying that she will tell him and that he will cut the penis off. Strange to say, this threat operates only if another condition is fulfilled before or afterwards. In itself it seems too inconceivable to the boy that such a thing could happen. But if at the time of the threat he can recall the appearance of female genitals or if shortly afterwards he has a sight of them—of genitals, that is to say, which really lack this supremely valued part, then he takes what he has heard seriously and, coming under the influence of the *castration complex*, experiences the severest trauma of his young life.[1]

The results of the threat of castration are multifarious and incalculable; they affect the whole of a boy's relations with his father and mother and subsequently with men and women in general. As a rule the child's masculinity is unable to stand up to this first shock. In order to preserve his sexual organ he renounces the possession of his mother more or less completely; his sexual life often remains permanently encumbered by the prohibition. If a strong feminine component, as we call it, is present in him, its strength is increased by this intimidation of his masculinity. He falls into a passive attitude to his father, such as he attributes to his mother. It is true that as a result of the threat he has given up masturbation, but not the activities of his imagination accompanying it. On the contrary, since these are now the only form of sexual satisfaction remaining to him, he indulges in them more than before and in these phantasies, though he still continues to identify himself with his father, he also does so, simultaneously and perhaps predominantly, with his mother. Derivatives and modified products of these early masturbatory phantasies usually make their way into his later ego and play a part in the formation of his character. Apart from this encouragement of his femininity, fear and hatred of his father gain greatly in intensity. The boy's masculinity withdraws, as it were, into a defiant attitude towards his father, which will dominate his later behaviour in human

[1] Castration has a place too in the Oedipus legend, for the blinding with which Oedipus punishes himself after the discovery of his crime is, by the evidence of dreams, a symbolic substitute for castration. The possibility cannot be excluded that a phylogenetic memory-trace may contribute to the extraordinarily terrifying effect of the threat—a memory-trace from the prehistory of the primal family, when the jealous father actually robbed his son of his genitals if the latter became troublesome to him as a rival with a woman. The primaeval custom of circumcision, another symbolic substitute for castration, can only be understood as an expression of submission to the father's will. (Cf. the puberty rites of primitive peoples.) No investigation has yet been made of the form taken by the events described above among peoples and in civilizations which do not suppress masturbation in children.

society in a compulsive fashion. A residue of his erotic fixation to his mother is often left in the form of an excessive dependence on her, and this persists as a kind of bondage to women.[1] He no longer ventures to love his mother, but he cannot risk not being loved by her, for in that case he would be in danger of being betrayed by her to his father and handed over to castration. The whole experience, with all its antecedents and consequences, of which my account has only been able to give a selection, is subjected to a highly energetic repression, and, as is made possible by the laws operating in the unconscious id, all the mutually contending emotional impulses and reactions which are set going at that time are preserved in the unconscious and ready to disturb the later development of the ego after puberty. When the somatic process of sexual maturation puts fresh life into the old libidinal fixations which had apparently been surmounted, sexual life will turn out to be inhibited, without homogeneity and fallen apart into mutually conflicting urges.

It is no doubt true that the impact of the threat of castration upon a boy's budding sexual life does not always have these dreaded consequences. It will depend once again on *quantitative* relations how much damage is done and how much avoided. The whole occurrence, which may probably be regarded as the central experience of the years of childhood, the greatest problem of early life and the strongest source of later inadequacy, is so completely forgotten that its reconstruction during the work of analysis is met in adults by the most decided disbelief. Indeed, aversion to it is so great that people try to silence any mention of the proscribed subject and the most obvious reminders of it are overlooked by a strange intellectual blindness. One may hear it objected, for instance, that the legend of King Oedipus has in fact no connection with the construction made by analysis: the cases are quite different, since Oedipus did not know that it was his father that he killed and his mother that he married. What is overlooked in this is that a distortion of this kind is inevitable if an attempt is made at a poetic handling of the material, and that there is no introduction of extraneous material but only a skilful employment of the factors presented by the theme. The ignorance of Oedipus is a legitimate representation of the unconscious state

[1] [Cf. a footnote to Section VIII of 'Analysis Terminable and Interminable' (1937*c*), *S.E.*, **23**, 252. See also p. 65 below.]

into which, for adults, the whole experience has fallen; and the coercive power of the oracle, which makes or should make the hero innocent, is a recognition of the inevitability of the fate which has condemned every son to live through the Oedipus complex. Again it was pointed out from psycho-analytic quarters how easily the riddle of another dramatic hero, Shakespeare's procrastinator, Hamlet, can be solved by reference to the Oedipus complex, since the prince came to grief over the task of punishing someone else for what coincided with the substance of his own Oedipus wish—whereupon the general lack of understanding on the part of the literary world showed how ready is the mass of mankind to hold fast to its infantile repressions.[1]

Yet more than a century before the emergence of psycho-analysis the French philosopher Diderot bore witness to the importance of the Oedipus complex by expressing the difference between the primitive and civilized worlds in this sentence: 'Si le petit sauvage était abandonné à lui-même, qu'il conservât toute son imbécillité, et qu'il réunît au peu de raison de l'enfant au berceau la violence des passions de l'homme de trente ans, il tordrait le col à son père et coucherait avec sa mère.'[2] I venture to say that if psycho-analysis could boast of no other

[1] The name 'William Shakespeare' is very probably a pseudonym behind which a great unknown lies concealed. Edward de Vere, Earl of Oxford, a man who has been thought to be identifiable with the author of Shakespeare's works, lost a beloved and admired father while he was still a boy and completely repudiated his mother, who contracted a new marriage very soon after her husband's death.—[Freud's first mention of this view was in a sentence added in 1930 to a footnote to Chapter V (D) of *The Interpretation of Dreams* (1900a), Standard Ed., **4**, 266 n. He enlarged on the point in his 'Address in the Goethe House' (1930e), ibid., **21**, 211, as well as in a footnote added in 1935 to his *Autobiographical Study* (1925d), ibid., **20**, 63–4 n. He referred to it once more in a footnote to Section A of Part I of the Third Essay in *Moses and Monotheism* (1939a), S.E., **23**, 65 n. A long argument in favour of this opinion is contained in a letter written by Freud to J. S. H. Branson on March 25, 1934, which is published in Appendix A (No. 27) to the third volume of Jones's biography (1957, 487–8).]

[2] ['If the little savage were left to himself, preserving all his foolishness and adding to the small sense of a child in the cradle the violent passions of a man of thirty, he would strangle his father and lie with his mother.' (From *Le neveu de Rameau*.) Freud had quoted this twice already. Cf. Lecture XXI of his *Introductory Lectures* (1916–17), Standard Ed., **16**, 337–8.]

achievement than the discovery of the repressed Oedipus complex, that alone would give it a claim to be included among the precious new acquisitions of mankind.

The effects of the castration complex in little girls are more uniform and no less profound. A female child has, of course, no need to fear the loss of a penis; she must, however, react to the fact of not having received one. From the very first she envies boys its possession; her whole development may be said to take place under the colours of envy for the penis. She begins by making vain attempts to do the same as boys and later, with greater success, makes efforts to compensate for her defect—efforts which may lead in the end to a normal feminine attitude. If during the phallic phase she tries to get pleasure like a boy by the manual stimulation of her genitals, it often happens that she fails to obtain sufficient satisfaction and extends her judgement of inferiority from her stunted penis to her whole self. As a rule she soon gives up masturbating, since she has no wish to be reminded of the superiority of her brother or playmate, and turns away from sexuality altogether.

If a little girl persists in her first wish—to grow into a boy—in extreme cases she will end as a manifest homosexual, and otherwise she will exhibit markedly masculine traits in the conduct of her later life, will choose a masculine vocation, and so on. The other path leads by way of abandoning the mother she has loved: the daughter, under the influence of her envy for the penis, cannot forgive her mother for having sent her into the world so insufficiently equipped. In her resentment over this she gives up her mother and puts someone else in her place as the object of her love—her father. If one has lost a love-object, the most obvious reaction is to identify oneself with it, to replace it from within, as it were, by identification. This mechanism now comes to the little girl's help. Identification with her mother can take the place of attachment to her mother. The little daughter puts herself in her mother's place, as she has always done in her games; she tries to take her mother's place with her father, and begins to hate the mother she used to love, and from two motives: from jealousy as well as from mortification over the penis she has been denied. Her new relation to her father may start by having as its content a wish to have his penis at her disposal, but it culminates in another wish—to have a baby from him as a gift. The wish for a baby has thus taken the place of the wish for a penis, or has at all events split off from it.

It is an interesting thing that the relation between the Oedipus complex and the castration complex should take such a different shape—an opposite one, in fact—in the case of females as compared to that of males. In males, as we have seen, the threat of castration brings the Oedipus complex to an end; in females we find that, on the contrary, it is their lack of a penis that forces them into their Oedipus complex. It does little harm to a woman if she remains in her feminine Oedipus attitude. (The term 'Electra complex' has been proposed for it.[1]) She will in that case choose her husband for his paternal characteristics and be ready to recognize his authority. Her longing to possess a penis, which is in fact unappeasable, may find satisfaction if she can succeed in completing her love for the organ by extending it to the bearer of the organ, just as happened earlier when she progressed from her mother's breast to her mother as a whole person.

If we ask an analyst what his experience has shown to be the mental structures least accessible to influence in his patients, the answer will be: in a woman her wish for a penis, in a man his feminine attitude towards his own sex, a precondition of which would, of course, be the loss of his penis.[2]

[1] [The term seems to have been used first by Jung (1913, 370). Freud argued against its introduction in his paper on 'Female Sexuality' (1931b), *Standard Ed.*, **21**, 229.]

[2] [Freud had discussed this at much greater length in Section VIII of 'Analysis Terminable and Interminable' (1937c), *S.E.*, **23**, 250 ff.]

PART III

THE THEORETICAL YIELD

CHAPTER VIII

THE PSYCHICAL APPARATUS AND THE EXTERNAL WORLD

ALL of the general discoveries and hypotheses which I brought forward in the first chapter were, of course, arrived at by laborious and patient detailed work of the kind of which I have given an example in the previous chapter. We may now feel tempted to make a survey of the increases in knowledge that we have achieved by work such as this and to consider what paths we have opened for further advances. In this connection we may be struck by the fact that we have so often been obliged to venture beyond the frontiers of the science of psychology. The phenomena with which we were dealing do not belong to psychology alone; they have an organic and biological side as well, and accordingly in the course of our efforts at building up psycho-analysis we have also made some important biological discoveries and have not been able to avoid framing new biological hypotheses.

But let us for the moment keep to psychology. We have seen that it is not scientifically feasible to draw a line of demarcation between what is psychically normal and abnormal; so that that distinction, in spite of its practical importance, possesses only a conventional value. We have thus established a right to arrive at an understanding of the normal life of the mind from a study of its disorders—which would not be admissible if these pathological states, neuroses and psychoses, had specific causes operating in the manner of foreign bodies.

The study of a mental disorder occurring during sleep, which is transient and harmless and which, indeed, performs a useful function, has given us a key to the understanding of the mental diseases which are permanent and injurious to life. And we may now venture on the assertion that the psychology of consciousness

was no better capable of understanding the normal functioning of the mind than of understanding dreams. The data of
conscious self-perception, which alone were at its disposal, have
proved in every respect inadequate to fathom the profusion and
complexity of the processes of the mind, to reveal their inter-
connections and so to recognize the determinants of their
disturbances.

The hypothesis we have adopted of a psychical apparatus
extended in space, expediently put together, developed by the
exigencies of life, which gives rise to the phenomena of consciousness only at one particular point and under certain conditions—this hypothesis has put us in a position to establish
psychology on foundations similar to those of any other science,
such, for instance, as physics. In our science as in the others the
problem is the same: behind the attributes (qualities) of the
object under examination which are presented directly to our
perception, we have to discover something else which is more
independent of the particular receptive capacity of our sense
organs and which approximates more closely to what may be
supposed to be the real state of affairs. We have no hope of
being able to reach the latter itself, since it is evident that everything new that we have inferred must nevertheless be translated back into the language of our perceptions, from which it is
simply impossible for us to free ourselves. But herein lies the
very nature and limitation of our science. It is as though we
were to say in physics: 'If we could see clearly enough we should
find that what appears to be a solid body is made up of particles
of such and such a shape and size and occupying such and such
relative positions.' In the meantime we try to increase the
efficiency of our sense organs to the furthest possible extent by
artificial aids; but it may be expected that all such efforts will
fail to affect the ultimate outcome. Reality will always remain
'unknowable'. The yield brought to light by scientific work
from our primary sense perceptions will consist in an insight
into connections and dependent relations which are present in
the external world, which can somehow be reliably reproduced
or reflected in the internal world of our thought and a knowledge of which enables us to 'understand' something in the
external world, to foresee it and possibly to alter it. Our procedure in psycho-analysis is quite similar. We have discovered
technical methods of filling up the gaps in the phenomena of

our consciousness, and we make use of those methods just as a physicist makes use of experiment. In this manner we infer a number of processes which are in themselves 'unknowable' and interpolate them in those that are conscious to us. And if, for instance, we say: 'At this point an unconscious memory intervened', what that means is: 'At this point something occurred of which we are totally unable to form a conception, but which, if it had entered our consciousness, could only have been described in such and such a way.'

Our justification for making such inferences and interpolations and the degree of certainty attaching to them of course remain open to criticism in each individual instance; and it cannot be denied that it is often extremely difficult to arrive at a decision—a fact which finds expression in the lack of agreement among analysts. The novelty of the problem is to blame for this—that is to say, a lack of training. But there is besides this a special factor inherent in the subject itself; for in psychology, unlike physics, we are not always concerned with things which can only arouse a cool scientific interest. Thus we shall not be very greatly surprised if a woman analyst who has not been sufficiently convinced of the intensity of her own wish for a penis also fails to attach proper importance to that factor in her patients. But such sources of error, arising from the personal equation, have no great importance in the long run. If one looks through old text-books on the use of the microscope, one is astonished to find the extraordinary demands which were made on the personality of those who made observations with that instrument while its technique was still young—of all of which there is no question to-day.

I cannot undertake to attempt a complete picture here of the psychical apparatus and its activities; I should find myself hindered, among other things, by the circumstance that psycho-analysis has not yet had time to study all those functions equally. I shall therefore content myself with a detailed recapitulation of the account in my opening chapter.

The core of our being, then, is formed by the obscure *id*, which has no direct communication with the external world and is accessible even to our own knowledge only through the medium of another agency. Within this id the organic *instincts* operate, which are themselves compounded of fusions of two primal forces (Eros and destructiveness) in varying proportions and are differentiated from one another by their relation to organs or systems of organs. The one and only urge of these instincts is towards satisfaction, which is expected to arise from certain changes in the organs with the help of objects in the external world. But immediate and unheeding satisfaction of the instincts, such as the id demands, would often lead to perilous conflicts with the external world and to extinction. The id knows no solicitude about ensuring survival and no anxiety; or it would perhaps be more correct to say that, though it can generate the sensory elements of anxiety, it cannot make use of them. The processes which are possible in and between the assumed psychical elements in the id (the *primary process*) differ widely from those which are familiar to us through conscious perception in our intellectual and emotional life; nor are they subject to the critical restrictions of logic, which repudiates some of these processes as invalid and seeks to undo them.

The id, cut off from the external world, has a world of perception of its own. It detects with extraordinary acuteness certain changes in its interior, especially oscillations in the tension of its instinctual needs, and these changes become conscious as feelings in the pleasure-unpleasure series. It is hard to say, to be sure, by what means and with the help of what sensory terminal organs these perceptions come about. But it is an established fact that self-perceptions—coenaesthetic feelings and feelings of pleasure-unpleasure—govern the passage of events in the id with despotic force. The id obeys the inexorable pleasure principle. But not the id alone. It seems that the activity of the other psychical agencies too is able only to modify the pleasure principle but not to nullify it; and it remains a question of the highest theoretical importance, and one that has not yet been answered, when and how it is ever possible for the pleasure principle to be overcome. The consideration that the pleasure principle demands a reduction, at bottom the extinction perhaps, of the tensions of instinctual needs (that is, *Nirvana*) leads to the still unassessed relations between the pleasure principle and the two primal forces, Eros and the death instinct.

The other agency of the mind, which we believe we know best and in which we recognize ourselves most easily—what is known as the *ego*—has been developed out of the id's cortical layer, which, through being adapted to the reception and exclusion of stimuli, is in direct contact with the external world (*reality*). Starting from conscious perception it has subjected to its influence ever larger regions and deeper strata of the id, and, in the persistence with which it maintains its dependence on the external world, it bears the indelible stamp of its origin (as it might be 'Made in Germany'[1]). Its psychological function consists in raising the passage [of events] in the id to a higher dynamic level (perhaps by transforming freely mobile energy into bound energy, such as corresponds to the preconscious state); its constructive function consists in interpolating, between the demand made by an instinct and the action that satisfies it, the activity of thought which, after taking its bearings in the present and assessing earlier experiences, endeavours by means of experimental actions to calculate the consequences of the course of action proposed. In this way the ego comes to a decision on whether the attempt to obtain satisfaction is to be carried out or postponed or whether it may not be necessary for the demand by the instinct to be suppressed altogether as being dangerous. (Here we have the *reality principle*.) Just as the id is directed exclusively to obtaining pleasure, so the ego is governed by considerations of safety. The ego has set itself the task of self-preservation, which the id appears to neglect. It [the ego] makes use of the sensations of anxiety as a signal to give a warning of dangers that threaten its integrity. Since memory-traces can become conscious just as perceptions do, especially through their association with residues of speech, the possibility arises of a confusion which would lead to a mistaking of reality. The ego guards itself against this possibility by the institution of *reality-testing*, which is allowed to fall into abeyance in dreams on account of the conditions prevailing in the state of sleep. The ego, which seeks to maintain itself in an environment of over-whelming mechanical forces, is threatened by dangers which come in the first instance from external reality; but dangers do not threaten it from there alone. Its own id is a source of similar dangers, and that for two different reasons. In the first place, an excessive strength of instinct can damage the ego in a similar way to an excessive 'stimulus' from the external world. It is true that the former cannot destroy it; but it can destroy its characteristic dynamic organization and change the ego back into a portion of the id. In the second place, experience may

[1] [In English in the original.]

have taught the ego that the satisfaction of some instinctual demand which is not in itself intolerable would involve dangers in the external world, so that an instinctual demand of that kind itself becomes a danger. Thus the ego is fighting on two fronts: it has to defend its existence against an external world which threatens it with annihilation as well as against an internal world that makes excessive demands. It adopts the same methods of defence against both, but its defence against the internal enemy is particularly inadequate. As a result of having originally been identical with this latter enemy and of having lived with it since on the most intimate terms, it has great difficulty in escaping from the internal dangers. They persist as threats, even if they can be temporarily held down.

We have heard how the weak and immature ego of the first period of childhood is permanently damaged by the stresses put upon it in its efforts to fend off the dangers that are peculiar to that period of life. Children are protected against the dangers that threaten them from the external world by the solicitude of their parents; they pay for this security by a fear of *loss of love* which would deliver them over helpless to the dangers of the external world. This factor exerts a decisive influence on the outcome of the conflict when a boy finds himself in the situation of the Oedipus complex, in which the threat to his narcissism by the danger of castration, reinforced from primaeval sources, takes possession of him. Driven by the combined operation of these two influences, the contemporary real danger and the remembered one with its phylogenetic basis, the child embarks on his attempts at defence—repressions—which are effective for the moment but nevertheless turn out to be psychologically inadequate when the later re-animation of sexual life brings a reinforcement to the instinctual demands which have been repudiated in the past. If this is so, it would have to be said from a biological standpoint that the ego comes to grief over the task of mastering the excitations of the early sexual period, at a time when its immaturity makes it incompetent to do so. It is in this lagging of ego development behind libidinal development that we see the essential precondition of neurosis; and we cannot escape the conclusion that neuroses could be avoided if the childish ego were spared this task—if, that is to say, the child's sexual life were allowed free play, as happens among many primitive peoples. It may be that the aetiology of neurotic illnesses is more complicated than we have here described it; if so, we have at least brought out one essential part of the aetiological complex. Nor should we forget the phylogenetic influences, which are represented in some way in the id in forms that we are not yet able to grasp, and which must certainly act upon the ego more powerfully in that early period than later. On the other hand, the realization dawns on us that such an early attempt at damming up the sexual instinct, so decided a partisanship by the young ego in favour of the external as opposed to the internal world, brought about by the prohibition of infantile sexuality, cannot be without its effect on the individual's later readiness for culture.[1] The instinctual demands forced away from direct satisfaction are compelled to enter on new paths leading to substitutive satisfaction, and in the course of these *détours* they may become desexualized and their connection with their original instinctual aims may become looser. And at this point we may anticipate the thesis that many of the highly valued assets of our civilization were acquired at the cost of sexuality and by the restriction of sexual motive forces.

We have repeatedly had to insist on the fact that the ego owes its origin as well as the most important of its acquired characteristics to its relation to the real external world. We are thus prepared to assume that the ego's pathological states, in which it most approximates once again to the id, are founded on a cessation or slackening of that relation to the external world. This tallies very well with what we learn from clinical experience—namely, that the precipitating cause of the outbreak of a psychosis is either that reality has become intolerably painful or that the instincts have become extraordinarily intensified— both of which, in view of the rival claims made on the ego by the id and the external world, must lead to the same result. The problem of psychoses would be simple and perspicuous if the ego's detachment from reality could be carried through completely. But that seems to happen only rarely or perhaps never. Even in a state so far removed from the reality of the external

---

[1] [The very similar concept of 'susceptibility to culture' had been discussed by Freud at some length in the first section of 'Thoughts for the Times on War and Death' (1915b), *Standard Ed.*, **14**, 283–4, and was also mentioned in *The Future of an Illusion* (1927c), ibid., **21**, 38; *I.P.L.* **15**, 34.—Freud made no distinction between the use of the words 'culture' and 'civilization'.]

world as one of hallucinatory confusion,[1] one learns from patients after their recovery that at the time in some corner of their mind (as they put it) there was a normal person hidden, who, like a detached spectator, watched the hubbub of illness go past him. I do not know if we may assume that this is so in general, but I can report the same of other psychoses with a less tempestuous course. I call to mind a case of chronic paranoia in which after each attack of jealousy a dream conveyed to the analyst a correct picture of the precipitating cause, free from any delusion.[2] An interesting contrast was thus brought to light: while we are accustomed to discover from the dreams of neurotics jealousies which are alien to their waking lives, in this psychotic case the delusion which dominated the patient in the day-time was corrected by his dream. We may probably take it as being generally true that what occurs in all these cases is a psychical *split*. Two psychical attitudes have been formed instead of a single one—one, the normal one, which takes account of reality, and another which under the influence of the instincts detaches the ego from reality. The two exist alongside of each other. The issue depends on their relative strength. If the second is or becomes the stronger, the necessary precondition for a psychosis is present. If the relation is reversed, then there is an apparent cure of the delusional disorder. Actually it has only retreated into the unconscious—just as numerous observations lead us to believe that the delusion existed ready-made for a long time before its manifest irruption.

The view which postulates that in all psychoses there is a *splitting of the ego* could not call for so much notice if it did not turn out to apply to other states more like the neuroses and, finally, to the neuroses themselves. I first became convinced of this in cases of *fetishism*. This abnormality, which may be counted as one of the perversions, is, as is well known, based on the patient (who is almost always male) not recognizing the fact that females have no penis—a fact which is extremely undesirable to him since it is a proof of the possibility of his being castrated himself. He therefore disavows his own sense-perception which showed him that the female genitals lack a penis and holds fast to the contrary conviction. The disavowed per-

[1] [Freud adds the term 'amentia', used by Meynert in this sense.]
[2] [This case is reported at some length in Freud's paper 'Some Neurotic Mechanisms' (1922b), *Standard Ed.*, **18**, 227.]

ception does not, however, remain entirely without influence, for, in spite of everything, he has not the courage to assert that he actually saw a penis. He takes hold of something else instead—a part of the body or some other object—and assigns it the role of the penis which he cannot do without. It is usually something that he in fact saw at the moment at which he saw the female genitals, or it is something that can suitably serve as a symbolic substitute for the penis. Now it would be incorrect to describe this process when a fetish is constructed as a splitting of the ego; it is a compromise formed with the help of displacement, such as we have been familiar with in dreams. But our observations show us still more. The creation of the fetish was due to an intention to destroy the evidence for the possibility of castration, so that fear of castration could be avoided. If females, like other living creatures, possess a penis, there is no need to tremble for the continued possession of one's own penis. Now we come across fetishists who have developed the same fear of castration as non-fetishists and react in the same way to it. Their behaviour is therefore simultaneously expressing two contrary premises. On the one hand they are disavowing the fact of their perception—the fact that they saw no penis in the female genitals; and on the other hand they are recognizing the fact that females have no penis and are drawing the correct conclusions from it. The two attitudes persist side by side throughout their lives without influencing each other. Here is what may rightly be called a splitting of the ego. This circumstance also enables us to understand how it is that fetishism is so often only partially developed. It does not govern the choice of object exclusively but leaves room for a greater or lesser amount of normal sexual behaviour; sometimes, indeed, it retires into playing a modest part or is limited to a mere hint. In festishists, therefore, the detachment of the ego from the reality of the external world has never succeeded completely.

It must not be thought that fetishism presents an exceptional case as regards a splitting of the ego; it is merely a particularly favourable subject for studying the question. Let us return to our thesis that the childish ego, under the domination of the real world, gets rid of undesirable instinctual demands by what are called repressions. We will now supplement this by further asserting that, during the same period of life, the ego often enough finds itself in the position of fending off some demand from the external world which it feels distressing and that this is effected by means of a *disavowal* of the perceptions which bring to knowledge this demand from reality. Disavowals of this kind occur very often and not only with fetishists; and whenever we are in a position to study them they turn out to be half-measures, incomplete attempts at detachment from reality. The disavowal is always supplemented by an acknowledgement; two contrary and independent attitudes always arise and result in the situation of there being a splitting of the ego. Once more the issue depends on which of the two can seize hold of the greater intensity.[1]

The facts of this splitting of the ego, which we have just described, are neither so new nor so strange as they may at first appear. It is indeed a universal characteristic of neuroses that there are present in the subject's mental life, as regards some particular behaviour, two different attitudes, contrary to each other and independent of each other. In the case of neuroses, however, one of these attitudes belongs to the ego and the contrary one, which is repressed, belongs to the id. The difference between this case and the other [discussed in the previous paragraph] is essentially a topographical or structural one, and it is not always easy to decide in an individual instance with which of the two possibilities one is dealing. They have, however, the following important characteristic in common. Whatever the ego does in its efforts of defence, whether it seeks to disavow a portion of the real external world or whether it seeks to reject an instinctual demand from the internal world, its success is never complete and unqualified. The outcome always lies in two contrary attitudes, of which the defeated, weaker one, no less than the other, leads to psychical complications. In conclusion, it is only necessary to point out how little of all these processes becomes known to us through our conscious perception.[2]

[1] [I.e., the greater psychical energy. See footnote, p. 25 above.]
[2] [The account of fetishism in this chapter is mainly derived from Freud's paper on the subject written some ten years before (1927*e*), where an early reference to a splitting of the ego will also be found. Cf. the Editor's Note to that paper, *Standard Ed.*, **19**, 150–1. Both these questions had also been approached in an unfinished paper 'Splitting of the Ego in the Process of Defence' (1940*e*) [1938], (*S.E.*, **23**, 271), which Freud had begun a few months before he wrote the present work. A discussion of the position appears in the Editor's Note to that paper, ibid., 273 f.]

Chapter IX

THE INTERNAL WORLD

WE have no way of conveying knowledge of a complicated set of simultaneous events except by describing them successively; and thus it happens that all our accounts are at fault to begin with owing to one-sided simplification and must wait till they can be supplemented, built on to, and so set right.

The picture of an ego which mediates between the id and the external world, which takes over the instinctual demands of the former in order to lead them to satisfaction, which derives perceptions from the latter and uses them as memories, which, intent on its self-preservation, puts itself in defence against excessively strong claims from both sides and which, at the same time, is guided in all its decisions by the injunctions of a modified pleasure principle—this picture in fact applies to the ego only up to the end of the first period of childhood, till about the age of five. At about that time an important change has taken place. A portion of the external world has, at least partially, been abandoned as an object and has instead, by identification, been taken into the ego and thus become an integral part of the internal world. This new psychical agency continues to carry on the functions which have hitherto been performed by the people [the abandoned objects] in the external world: it observes the ego, gives it orders, judges it and threatens it with punishments, exactly like the parents whose place it has taken. We call this agency the *super-ego* and are aware of it in its judicial functions as our *conscience*. It is a remarkable thing that the super-ego often displays a severity for which no model has been provided by the real parents, and moreover that it calls the ego to account not only for its deeds but equally for its thoughts and unexecuted intentions, of which the super-ego seems to have knowledge. This reminds us that the hero of the Oedipus legend too felt guilty for his deeds and submitted himself to self-punishment, although the coercive power of the oracle should have acquitted him of guilt in our judgement and his own. The super-ego is in fact the heir to the Oedipus complex and is only established after that complex has been disposed of.

For that reason its excessive severity does not follow a real model but corresponds to the strength of the defence used against the temptation of the Oedipus complex. Some suspicion of this state of things lies, no doubt, at the bottom of the assertion made by philosophers and believers that the moral sense is not instilled into men by education or acquired by them in their social life but is implanted in them from a higher source.

So long as the ego works in full harmony with the super-ego it is not easy to distinguish between their manifestations; but tensions and estrangements between them make themselves very plainly visible. The torments caused by the reproaches of conscience correspond precisely to a child's fear of loss of love, a fear the place of which has been taken by the moral agency. On the other hand, if the ego has successfully resisted a temptation to do something which would be objectionable to the super-ego, it feels raised in its self-esteem and strengthened in its pride, as though it had made some precious acquisition. In this way the super-ego continues to play the part of an external world for the ego, although it has become a portion of the internal world. Throughout later life it represents the influence of a person's childhood, of the care and education given him by his parents and of his dependence on them—a childhood which is prolonged so greatly in human beings by a family life in common. And in all this it is not only the personal qualities of these parents that is making itself felt, but also everything that had a determining effect on them themselves, the tastes and standards of the social class in which they lived and the innate dispositions and traditions of the race from which they sprang. Those who have a liking for generalizations and sharp distinctions may say that the external world, in which the individual finds himself exposed after being detached from his parents, represents the power of the present; that his id, with its inherited trends, represents the organic past; and that the super-ego, which comes to join them later, represents more than anything the cultural past, which a child has, as it were, to repeat as an after-experience during the few years of his early life. It is unlikely that such generalizations can be universally correct. Some portion of the cultural acquisitions have undoubtedly left a precipitate behind them in the id; much of what is contributed by the super-ego will awaken an echo in the id; not a few of the child's new experiences will be intensified because they are repetitions of some primaeval phylogenetic experience.

> 'Was du ererbt von deinen Vätern hast,
> Erwirb es, um es zu besitzen.'[1]

Thus the super-ego takes up a kind of intermediate position between the id and the external world; it unites in itself the influences of the present and the past. In the establishment of the super-ego we have before us, as it were, an example of the way in which the present is changed into the past. . . .

* * * * *

[1] ['What thou hast inherited from thy fathers, acquire it to make it thine.' Goethe, *Faust*, Part I, Scene 1.—Freud had quoted this previously in his *Totem and Taboo* (1912–13), *Standard Ed.*, **13**, 158.]

ADDENDA

Page 10, line 18 [The German word translated here by 'hominization' is '*Menschwerdung*', 'the process of becoming
human'. The topic was also mentioned by Freud in
Moses and Monotheism (1939*a*), Essay III, Part I,
Section C (1), *Standard Ed.*, **23**, 75.]

26, line 17 [Cf. 'The Antithetical Meaning of Primal Words'
(1910*e*), *Standard Ed.*, **11**, 159. The point is raised
again in *Moses and Monotheism*, (1939*a*), Essay III,
Part II, Section D, *Standard Ed.*, **23**, 121.]

48 *n.* [The state of sexual 'bondage' in men had also
been alluded to by Freud in his paper on 'The
Taboo of Virginity' (1918*a*), *Standard Ed.*, **11**, 194.]

LIST OF ABBREVIATIONS

G.S. = Freud, *Gesammelte Schriften* (12 vols.), Vienna 1924–34

G.W. = Freud, *Gesammelte Werke* (18 vols.), London, from 1940, Frankfurt am Main, from 1960

C.P. = Freud, *Collected Papers* (5 vols.), London, 1924–50

S.E.
Standard Ed. } = Freud, *Standard Edition* (24 vols.), London, from 1953

I.P.L. = *International Psycho-Analytical Library*, Hogarth Press and Institute of Psycho-Analysis, London, from 1921

N. = Freud, Works published by W. W. Norton & Company Inc., New York

BIBLIOGRAPHY
AND AUTHOR INDEX

[Titles of books and periodicals are in italics; titles of papers are in inverted commas. Abbreviations are in accordance with the *World List of Scientific Periodicals* (London, 1963–5). Further abbreviations used in this volume will be found in the List on page 66. Numerals in thick type refer to volumes; ordinary numerals refer to pages. The figures in round brackets at the end of each entry indicate the page or pages of this volume on which the work in question is mentioned. In the case of the Freud entries, the letters attached to the date of publication are in accordance with the corresponding entries in the complete bibliography of Freud's writings to be included in the last volume of the *Standard Edition*.

For non-technical authors, and for technical authors where no specific work is mentioned, see the General Index.]

FERENCZI, S. (1913) 'Entwicklungsstufen des Wirklichkeitssinnes', *Int. Z. ärztl. Psychoanal.*, **1**, 124. (10)
  [*Trans.*: 'Stages in the Development of the Sense of Reality', *First Contributions to Psycho-Analysis*, London, 1952, Chap. VIII.]

FREUD, S. (1893h) Vortrag 'Über den psychischen Mechanismus hysterischer Phänomene' [shorthand report revised by lecturer], *Wien. med. Presse*, **34**, Nr. 4, 121, and 5, 165. (7)
  [*Trans.*: Lecture 'On the Psychical Mechanism of Hysterical Phenomena', *Int. J. Psycho-Analysis*, **37**, 8; *Standard Ed.* **3**, 27.]

  (1894a) 'Die Abwehr-Neuropsychosen', *G.S.*, **1**, 290; *G.W.*, **1**, 59. (25)
  [*Trans.*: 'The Neuro-Psychoses of Defence', *C.P.*, **1**, 59; *Standard Ed.*, **3**, 43.]

  (1900a) *Die Traumdeutung*, Vienna. *G.S.*, **2–3**; *G.W.*, **2–3**. (xi, 17, 49)
  [*Trans.*: *The Interpretation of Dreams*, London and New York, 1955; *Standard Ed.*, **4–5**.]

  (1905c) *Der Witz und seine Beziehung zum Unbewussten*, Vienna. *G.S.*, **9**, 5; *G.W.*, **6**. (15)
  [*Trans.*: *Jokes and their Relation to the Unconscious*, London and New York, 1960; *Standard Ed.*, **8**.]

  (1905d) *Drei Abhandlungen zur Sexualtheorie*, Vienna. *G.S.*, **5**, 3; *G.W.*, **5**, 29. (6)
  [*Trans.*: *Three Essays on the Theory of Sexuality*, New York, 1965; *Standard Ed.*, **7**, 125; *I.P.L.*, **57**.]

  (1910e) ' "Über den Gegensinn der Urworte" ', *G.S.*, **10**, 221; *G.W.*, **8**, 214. (65)
  [*Trans.*: ' "The Antithetical Meaning of Primal Words" ', *C.P.*, **4**, 184; *Standard Ed.*, **11**, 155.]

  (1912–13) *Totem und Tabu*, Vienna, 1913. *G.S.*, **10**, 3; *G.W.*, **9**. (64)

FREUD, S. (*cont.*)

[*Trans.: Totem and Taboo*, London, 1960; New York, 1962; Standard Ed., **13**, 1.]

(1915*b*) 'Zeitgemässes über Krieg und Tod', *G.S.*, **10**, 315; *G.W.*, **10**, 324. (58)

[*Trans.*: 'Thoughts for the Times on War and Death', *C.P.*, **4**, 288; *Standard Ed.*, **14**, 275.]

(1915*e*) 'Das Unbewusste', *G.S.*, **5**, 480; *G.W.*, **10**, 264. (xi, 17)

[*Trans.*: 'The Unconscious', *C.P.*, **4**, 98; *Standard Ed.*, **14**, 161.]

(1916–17) *Vorlesungen zur Einführung in die Psychoanalyse*, Vienna. *G.S.*, **7**; *G.W.*, **11**. (49)

[*Trans.: Introductory Lectures on Psycho-Analysis*, London, 1929; revised ed., New York, 1966; *Standard Ed.*, **15–16.**]

(1918*a*) 'Das Tabu der Virginität', *G.S.*, **5**, 212; *G.W.*, **12**, 161. (65)

[*Trans.*: 'The Taboo of Virginity', *C.P.*, **4**, 217; *Standard Ed.*, **11**, 193.]

(1920*g*) *Jenseits des Lustprinzips*, Vienna. *G.S.*, **6**, 191; *G.W.*, **13**, 3. (6)

[*Trans.: Beyond the Pleasure Principle*, New York, 1959; *Standard Ed.*, **18**, 7; *I.P.L.*, **4.**]

(1922*b*) Über einige neurotische Mechanismen bei Eifersucht, Paranoia und Homosexualität', *G.S.*, **5**, 387; *G.W.*, **13**, 195. (59)

[*Trans.*: 'Some Neurotic Mechanisms in Jealousy, Paranoia and Homosexuality', *C.P.*, **2**, 232; *Standard Ed.*, **18**, 223.]

(1923*b*) *Das Ich und das Es*, Vienna, *G.S.*, **6**. 353; *G.W.*, **13**, 237. (xi, 8, 10)

[*Trans.: The Ego and the Id*, New York, 1962; *Standard Ed.*, **19**, 3; *I.P.L.*, **12.**]

(1925*d* [1924]) *Selbstdarstellung*, Vienna, 1934. *G.S.*, **11**, 119; *G.W.*, **14**, 33. (49)

[*Trans.: An Autobiographical Study*, London, 1935; New York, 1952; *Standard Ed.*, **20**, 3.]

(1926*d*) *Hemmung, Sympton und Angst*, Vienna. *G.S.*, **11**, 23; *G.W.*, **14**, 113. (10)

[*Trans.: Inhibitions, Symptoms and Anxiety, Standard Ed.*, **20**, 77; *I.P.L.*, **28.** (*The Problem of Anxiety*, New York, 1936.)]

(1927*c*) *Die Zukunft einer Illusion*, Vienna. *G.S.*, **11**, 411; *G.W.*, **14**, 325. (58)

[*Trans.: The Future of an Illusion*, New York, 1928; *Standard Ed.*, **21**, 3; *I.P.L.*, **15.**]

(1927*e*) 'Fetischismus', *G.S.*, **11**, 395; *G.W.*, **14**, 311. (61)

[*Trans.*: 'Fetishism', *C.P.*, **5**, 198, *Standard Ed.*, **21**, 149.]

(1930*a*) *Das Unbehagen in der Kultur*, Vienna. *G.S.*, **12**, 29; *G.W.*, **14**, 421. (10)

[*Trans.: Civilization and its Discontents*, New York, 1961; *Standard Ed.*, **21**, 59; *I.P.L.*, **17.**]

(1930*e*) Ansprache im Frankfurter Goethe-Haus, *G.S.*, **12**, 408; *G.W.*, **14**, 547. (49)

[*Trans.*: Address delivered in the Goethe House at Frankfurt, *Standard Ed.*, **21**, 208.]

(1931*b*) 'Über die weibliche Sexualitat', *G.S.*, **12**, 120; *G.W.*, **14**, 517. (25, 51)

[*Trans.*: 'Female Sexuality', *C.P.*, **5**, 252; *Standard Ed.*, **21**, 223.]

(1933*a*) *Neue Folge der Vorlesungen zur Einführung in die Psychoanalyse*, Vienna. *G.S.*, **12**, 151; *G.W.*, **15**, 207.(6)

[*Trans.*: *New Introductory Lectures on Psycho-Analysis*, London, 1933; revised ed., New York, 1966; *Standard Ed.*, **22**, 3.]

(1933*b* [1932]) *Warum Krieg?* Paris, *G.S.*, **12**, 349; *G.W.*, **16**, 13. (6)

[*Trans.*: *Why War?* Paris, 1933; *C.P.*, **5**, 273; *Standard Ed.*, **22**, 197.]

(1937*c*) 'Die endliche und die unendliche Analyse', *G.W.*, **16**, 59. (6, 48, 51)

[*Trans.*: 'Analysis Terminable and Interminable', *C.P.*, **5**, 316; *Standard Ed.*, **23**, 211.]

(1939*a* [1937–39]) *Der Mann Moses und die monotheistische Religion*, *G.W.*, **16**, 103. (17, 49, 65)

[*Trans.*: *Moses and Monotheism*, London and New York, 1939; *Standard Ed.*, **23**, 3.]

(1940*a*) [1938] *Abriss der Psychoanalyse*, *G.W.*, **17**, 67.

[*Trans.*: *An Outline of Psycho-Analysis*, New York, 1968; *Standard Ed.*, **23**, 141; *I.P.L.*, **35**.]

(1940*b* [1938]) 'Some Elementary Lessons in Psycho-Analysis' [title in English: German text], *G.W.*, **17**, 141. (ix, x)

[*Trans.*: 'Some Elementary Lessons in Psycho-Analysis', *C.P.*, **5**, 376; *Standard Ed.*, **23**, 281.]

(1940*e* [1938]) 'Die Ichspaltung im Abwehrvorgang', *G.W.*, **17**, 59. (61)

[*Trans.*: 'Splitting of the Ego in the Process of Defence', *C.P.*, **5**, 372; *Standard Ed.*, **23**, 273.]

(1950*a* [1887–1902]) *Aus den Anfängen der Psychoanalyse*, London. Includes 'Entwurf einer Psychologie' (1895). (17, 25)

[*Trans.*: *The Origins of Psycho-Analysis*, London and New York, 1954. (Partly, including 'A Project for a Scientific Psychology', in *Standard Ed.*, **1**, 175.]

JONES, E. (1957) *Sigmund Freud: Life and Work*, Vol. 3, London and New York. (Page references are to the English edition.) (x, 49)

JUNG, C. G. (1913) 'Versuch einer Darstellung der psychoanalytischen Theorie', *Jb. psychoanalyt. psychopath. Forsch.*, **5**, 307. (51)

[*Trans.*: *The Theory of Psycho-Analysis*, New York, 1915.]

GENERAL INDEX

This index includes the names of non-technical authors. It also includes the names of technical authors where no reference is made in the text to specific works. For references to specific technical works, the Bibliography should be consulted.

Active and passive (*see also* Passive sexual attitude), 45
Affect, 14
Aggressiveness, 6–7, 11
Ambivalence
  of relation to father, 33
  of transference, 32–4
Amentia, 59 *n.* 1
Amnesia, infantile, 10, 43, 48
Anal erotism (*see* Sadistic-anal phase)
Analogies
  amoeba and pseudopodia, 7–8
  civil war, 30
  governors of conquered country, 24
  'Made in Germany', 56
  microscope, use of, 54
  N.C.O. reprimanded by superior officer, 25 *n.* 2
  nightwatchman, 28
  prick of needle during cell-division, 42
Animal ancestry of human beings, 43
Animals compared to human beings, 4, 10 *n.*, 19
Anticathexes, 22–3, 29, 35
Antithetical meaning of primal words, 26, 65
Anxiety (*see also* Fear), 40, 55
  as danger signal, 3, 5, 56
Anxiety dreams, 27–8
Archaic heritage, 24, 45, 47 n., 57–8, 63–4
Auditory perception, 19
Auto-erotism (*see* Masturbation)

Behaviourism, 14 *n.*
Birth, infantile theories of, 11
Bisexuality, 45
Blinding as symbol of castration, 47n.
Boys'
  relation to father, 33, 46–7
  relation to mother, 12, 46–8
  sexual development, 11–12, 45–9, 51, 57
Brain, anatomy of, 1–2
Branson, J. S. H., 50 *n.* 1
Breast (*see* Suckling and breast)

Castration
  complex, 12, 47–8, 50–1, 57, 59–60
  symbols of, 47 and *n.*
  threat, 12, 46–8, 51, 57
Character traits, 12, 47
Childhood (*see also* Infantile)
  dependence of, 3–4, 42, 44, 57, 63
  impressions, 23
Children (*see also* Parents and children)
  neuroses of, 41
  sexual abuse of, 44
  sexual researches of, 11
  sexual theories of, 11
Circumcision as symbol of castration, 47
Civilization, 42, 46, 58
Clitoris, 11 *n.* 2, 12
Cloacal theory of birth, 11
Component instincts, 8–12, 43
Compromises, dreams as, 26–7, 60
Condensation in dreams, 24–5
Conflicts, instinctual (*see* Instinctual conflicts)
Confusional states, 59
Conscience, 62–3
Consciousness
  nature of, 14–19, 53
  relation to brain, 1–2
  relation to ego, 18–19, 22, 36
  relation to preconscious, 17–19
  relation to unconscious, 16–18
Creative literature, 6 *n.* 1, 48

Danger
  anxiety as signal of, 3, 5, 56
  avoidance of, 3, 5, 56–7

Day's residues and dreams, 27
Death instinct, 5–7, 11 and *n*. 1, 37, 43, 54–5
Defence mechanisms (*see also* Ego and defence), 57
Degeneracy, 9
Delusions, psychotic, 29, 59
Destructiveness (*see* Death instinct)
Diderot, D., 49
Diphasic onset of sexual function, 10, 43
'Disavowal', 61
Displacement
  in dreams, 24–5, 60
  of instinctual aim, 5, 12
Distortion
  in creative literature, 48
  in dreams, 22, 24, 28
Dream-content, manifest, 22, 24–6
Dream-interpretation, 22–8, 34, 53
Dreams
  anxiety, 27–8
  as compromises, 26–7, 60
  characteristics of, 22
  childhood impressions as source of, 23
  compared to symptoms, 28–9, 60
  condensation in, 24–5
  day's residues and, 27
  displacement in, 24–5, 60
  distortion in, 22, 24, 28
  hallucinatory nature of, 19, 22, 56
  instinctual demands expressed in, 23–4, 26
  of neurotics, 59
  of psychotics, 59
  relaxation of resistance in, 18
  secondary revision of, 24
  sleep and, 22–3, 26–8
  symbolism of, 23, 26
  waking life and, 23–4, 26–8
  wish-fulfilment in, 23, 27–8
Dream-thoughts, latent, 22, 24–6
Dream-work, 22, 24–8
Dynamic view of mental processes, 13

Economic factors in mental processes (*see* Quantitative factors)
Ego
  alteration of, 29–30, 36–8
  and consciousness, 18–19, 22, 36
  and defence, 57, 60–1
  and external world, xi, 3, 5, 20, 23, 29–30, 37, 56–63

and id, 2–6, 20–3, 29, 34–8, 43, 55–8, 62
and instincts, 23–4, 26–8, 56–7, 59–62
and the preconscious, 19–21
and super-ego, 3, 22, 29, 34, 62–63
and the unconscious, 19
as reservoir of libido, 7–8
immature, 57–8, 60
later development of, 12, 47–8
neuroses as disorders of, 41–2, 57
principal characteristics of, 2–5, 19, 55–6
repressive forces of, 42
splitting of, xi, 59–61
strengthened by psycho-analysis, 30–7
Einstein, A., 6 *n*. 2
Electra complex, 51
Empedocles of Acragas, 6 *n*. 2
England, *Freud* in, x
Eros (*see also* Libido; Sexual instinct), 5–8, 43, 54–5
Erotogenic zones, 8–10
Errors, 19
Ethics, 63
Excretory functions, 11
External world
  adaptation to, 7, 13
  detachment from, in neurosis and psychosis, 19, 58–9
  ego's relation to, xi, 3, 5, 20, 23, 29–30, 37, 56–63
  id and, 2, 54–6
  super-ego and, 64
  'unknowable', 53–4

Father (*see also* Parents and children)
  ambivalent relation to, 33
  and castration threat, 46–8
  boy's relation to, 33, 46–7
  girl's relation to, 50
Faust (Goethe), 64
Fear (*see also* Anxiety)
  of castration (*see* Castration complex)
  of loss of love, 57, 63
Fetish equated with missing female penis, 59–60
Fetishism, xi, 59–61, 61 *n*. 2
Fixation of libido, 8, 10, 12, 38, 48
Fixierung, uses of word, 17 *n*.
Fliess, W., 17 *n*.
Fore-pleasure, 12

Free association, 26, 34
Freud, Sigmund, in England, x

Genitals
  and sexual instinct, 9
  female, and castration fear, 47, 59–60
  primacy of, 11–13
Girls'
  relation to father, 50
  relation to mother, 50–1
  sexual development, 12, 45, 50–1
Glacial epoch, 10 *n.*
Goethe, 64
Greek myths (*see* Oedipus)
Guilt, sense of, x, 62
  in neurotics, 36–8

Hallucinations, 19
Hallucinatory
  character of dreams, 19, 22, 56
  confusion, 59
Hamlet, 49
Hereditary factors (*see also* Archaic heritage), 2, 4, 40–1, 63
Hominization, 10, 65
Homosexuality, 9, 12, 50–1
Hunger as dream-instigator, 27
Hypercathexis, 21

Id, the
  and ego, 2–6, 20–3, 29, 34–8, 43, 55–8, 62
  and heredity, 2, 4, 63
  and repression, 20, 22, 35, 48, 61
  and the super-ego, 3–4, 63–4
  and the unconscious, 20–5, 28, 48
  instinctual demands of, 2–3, 5, 26, 29–30, 54–6
  principal characteristics of, 2, 5
  uncovered by psycho-analysis, 2 *n.* 2
Identification, xi, 47, 50
Ill, wish to be, 36–8
Impotence, sexual, 6
Infantile (*see also* Childhood; Children)
  amnesia, 10, 43, 48
  sexuality, 9–11, 43, 57–8
Inhibitions, 12, 23, 48
Instincts (*see also* Component instincts; Death instinct; Eros; Nutrition, instinct of; Self-preservative instinct; Sexual instinct)

ego and, 23–4, 26–8, 56–7, 59–62
  renunciation of, 12, 36, 42–3, 56–58, 61–2
  strength of, and aetiology of neurosis, 38, 40–3, 56–7
  theory of, 16
Instinctual
  aim, displacement of, 5, 12
  conflicts, 7
  demands of the id, 2–3, 5, 26, 29–30, 54–6
  impulses and dreams, 23–4, 26
Interpretation of dreams (*see* Dream-interpretation)

Jealousy, 10, 46, 47 *n.*
  delusional, 59
Jocasta, 44, 48
Jokes, 18

Kissing, 5

Laius, 44, 48
Latency period in childhood, 10 and *n.*, 12, 43
Legends (*see also* Tradition), 24
  of *Oedipus,* 44, 46, 47 *n.*, 48, 62
Libido
  defined, 6–8
  development of, 11–14, 57
  ego as reservoir of, 7–8
  fixation of, 8, 10, 12, 38, 48
  narcissistic, 7
  object-, 5, 7–8
  periodicity of, 10 *n.*
Life-instinct (*see* Eros)
Linguistic usage, 23
Lipps, T., 15
Literature, creative, 6 *n.* 1, 48
Love
  being in, 8, 33
  fear of loss of, 57, 63

Masculine and feminine, 45
Masochism, 11 *n.* 1
Masturbation, 12, 46–7, 50
  phantasies, 47
Memory (*see also* Amnesia), perception and, 62
Memory-traces, xi, 19, 56
  unconscious, 54
Men, sexual development of (*see* Boys')
Menstruation, 9 *n.*, 43
Meynert, T., 59 *n.* 1

Mind and body, relation between, 5, 14–15, 18–19
Morality, 63
Mother
  child's attachment to, 45–51
  child's identification with, 47, 50
  girl's hostility to, 50
Motility, 2, 7, 23
Myths (*see also* Legends), symbolism of, 47

Narcissism, primary, 5, 7, 45, 57
Narcissistic libido, 7
Neuronal activity, primary principle of, 25 *n.* 2
  aetiology of, 10, 40–4, 57–8
  and pressure of civilization, 42
  and trauma, 37, 41–2
  curability of, 29–32, 37–9
  of children, 41
Neurotic symptoms (*see* Symptoms)
Neurotics
  compared to normal persons, 13, 22, 40–1
  psycho-analysis of, 23
Neveu de Rameau, Le (by *Diderot*), 49, *n.* 2
Nirvana, 55
Normal persons compared to neurotics, 13, 22, 40–1
Nutrition, instinct of, 6, 11, 45

Object-choice, xi, 13, 45, 50
  in fetishism, 60
Object-libido, 5, 7–8
Oedipus
  complex, 12, 44, 46, 49–51, 57, 62–3
  legend, 44, 46, 47 *n.*, 48, 62
Oedipus Rex (by *Sophocles*), 44
Oral erotic phase, 10–12
Organic illness, 37
Oxford, Edward de Vere, Earl of, 49 *n.* 1

Pain, 18, 40, 58
Paranoia, 59
Parapraxes, 34
Parents
  analyst as successor to, 32–3, 38
  and children (*see also* Father; Mother), 3, 42, 47, 57, 63
  super-ego as successor to, 3–4, 32, 42, 62–3

Passive sexual attitude, 45, 47, 51
Penis (*see also* Phallic phase; Castration), 11 *n.* 2, 12, 46–7
  attributed to females, in fetishism, 59–60
  -envy, 12, 50–1, 54
Perceptual system, 2, 14, 16–19, 53, 55–6, 62
Periodicity, sexual, 10 *n.*, 43
Perversion (*see also* Fetishism), 9, 12, 44
Phallic phase, 11–12, 46, 50
Phantasies
  masturbation, 47
  primal, 46
  sexual, 12
Philosophy and psycho-analysis, 15–16
Phylogenetic heritage (*see* Archaic heritage)
Plato, 6, *n.* 1
Pleasure principle, 3, 11, 55, 62
Preconscious, 17–24, 27, 38
  and speech, xi, 19, 56
Preservation of the species, 14, 43
Primal
  phantasies, 46
  scene, 44
Primary process, 21, 25, 55
Psychical
  apparatus, 2–4, 14–21, 40, 53–62
  energy, 16, 20–21, 25, 56, 61 *n.* 1
Psycho-analysis
  and biology, 52
  and philosophy, 15–16
  and science, 15–16, 20, 53–4
  criticisms of, 54
  findings of, 1, 9, 21, 44, 51
  fundamental rule of, 31, 33, 36
  of neurotics, 23
  resistance to, 34–8
  restores forgotten experiences, 48
  technique of, 10, 16, 29–39, 53–4
  therapeutic aspect of, 30–9
  uncovers what is hidden in the id, 2 *n.* 2
Psychoneuroses (*see* Neuroses)
Psychosis, 18, 28–30, 40, 52, 58–9
  precipitating cause of, 58–9
Puberty, 9–10, 12, 48
Punishment, 42

Quantitative or economic factors, 13, 29, 38–41, 48

Reality (*see also* External world)
  -principle, 56
  -testing, 19, 56
Regression 13
Repression
  and the id, 20, 22, 35, 48, 61
  and resistance to psycho-analysis, 35–6
  and the unconscious, 22–3, 35, 38, 48–9
  as exclusion from consciousness, 17–18
  by the ego, 42
  of instinctual impulses, 12, 42–3, 57
  of traumatic memories, 44
Reproductive function, 9, 14, 43–4
Resistance
  repression as, 17–18
  to psycho-analysis, 34–8
Roux, W., 42

Sadistic-anal phase, 11–12
Science and psycho-analysis, 15–16, 20, 53–4
Secondary process, 21
Secondary revision of dreams, 24
Seduction, sexual, 44–5
Self-preservative instinct, 2, 5, 11, 37, 43, 56, 62
Sensory perception (*see* Perceptual system)
Sensory stimuli, 2–3, 16, 55–6
  auditory, 19
  visual, 19
Sexual
  act (*see also* Primal scene), 6, 27
  aim, 12–13
  bondage, 48, 65
  excitation, 43, 46
  function, diphasic onset of, 10, 43
  impotence, 6
  instinct (*see also* Eros), x, 8–14, 43–4, 58
  periodicity, 9 *n.*, 43
  phantasies, 12
  researches of children, 11
  seduction, 44–5
  theories of children, 11
Shakespeare, 49
Sleep, 3, 18, 22–3, 26–8, 52, 56
Social organization of man, 3, 37
Sophocles, 44
Speech, 19, 23, 56
  and the preconscious, xi, 19, 56
Stimuli (*see* Sensory stimuli)

Sublimation, 12, 38
Suckling and breast, 11, 45–6, 51
Suggestion, 33
Suicidal impulses, 7, 37
Super-ego, 5, 7
  and ego, 3, 22, 29, 34, 62–3
  and id, 3–4, 63–4
  equated with conscience, 30, 62
  partly unconscious, 19
  represents cultural past, 63
  severity of, 37–8, 62
  successor to Oedipus complex, 62–3
  successor to parents, 3–4, 32, 42, 62–3
Symbol of castration, 47
Symbolism
  of dreams, 23, 26
  of myths, 47
Symposium (of *Plato*), 6 *n.* 1
Symptoms, neurotic
  as substitute satisfactions, 43, 58
  incubation period of, 41
  removed by psycho-analysis, 32

Thought-processes, 14, 16, 19, 53, 56
Topographical view of mental processes, 18, 61
Tradition, 3
Transference, 31–4, 36, 38
  ambivalence of, 32–4
Trauma
  and aetiology of neurosis, 37, 41–2
  castration fear as, 12, 47
Traumatic neurosis, 41

Unconscious, the
  and repression, 22–3, 35, 38, 48–9
  relation to consciousness, 16–18
  relation to ego, 19
Unconscious
  memory-traces, 54
  mental processes, 15–31, 35–6, 38, 43, 48
  wish, 23
Unpleasure, 3, 40

Vagina, 11 and *n.* 2
Visual perceptions, 19

Waking life and dreams, 23–4, 26–8
Weaning, 46
Wish, unconscious, 23
Wish-fulfilment in dreams, 23, 27–8
Womb, sleep as return to, 23
Women, sexual development of (*see* Girls')